I0181776

SABRINA FISHER REECE

Kicking Depression in the Butt

How to Battle the Enemy Head On and Win

First published by In59Seconds Publishing 2025

Copyright © 2025 by SaBrina Fisher Reece

All rights reserved. No part of this publication may be reproduced, stored, or transmitted in any form or by any means, electronic, mechanical, photocopying, recording, scanning, or otherwise without written permission from the publisher. It is illegal to copy this book, post it to a website, or distribute it by any other means without permission.

No part of this book may be reproduced, stored in a retrieval system or transmitted in any form or by any means without the prior written permission of the publisher – except by a reviewer who may quote brief passages in a review to be printed in a newspaper, magazine or journal. For inquiry contact the publisher: In59Seconds@yahoo.com SoundWithSaBrina@yahoo.com

First edition

Cover art by SaBrina Fisher Reece

This book was professionally typeset on Reedsy. Find out more at reedsy.com

This book is for everyone man, woman or child that has suffered with depression. I know the pain of it personally. I want you to know that you can and you will live a life free from it. It is possible! I am a living witness that there is light on the other side of darkness. Please do not give up. Life gets better but you must commit to doing the mental and emotional work necessary to live a better quality of life. You are Great and it time to remember that. I love you
-SaBrina Fisher Reece

Contents

1

Recognizing the Enemy

What does Depression Really Feels Like? I personally know the feeling very well. When you are depressed you feel hopeless and unloved. You feel that God is not listening or helping you. It can feel that no one understands you and you are all alone in the world. I must first tell you that all of those feelings are valid, and although it may not seem like it at the time. Those feelings of doom and despair will pass. Before you read any further I want you to know that there is hope. I have to ensure you that, you will feel better one day. After darkness there will be light. So Please do not give up.

Depression isn't always loud. Sometimes it whispers. Sometimes it doesn't even feel like sadness at first. It feels like heaviness. Like a heavy weight is sitting on your chest. Like your spirit is wearing wet clothes you can't peel off. It feels like waking up already tired, like your body showed up but your joy forgot to come with you. It feels like moving through life underwater, people are talking, time is passing, responsibilities are stacking, and you're trying to act normal while your insides are quietly screaming, *"I can't do this."*

In my early twenties, I experienced depression many times. However, I didn't have a name for it. I was a young Black girl from Compton, California, who had two substance abusers as parents. My father's name was Jesse Paul Fisher, and he loved me and my sister the best he could, but he loved alcohol just a little bit more. He died of alcohol-related illnesses when I was ten years old.

My mother, on the other hand, never seemed to love me or any of the six children she gave birth to. My sister Mary and I were the oldest. Fortunately, we were raised by our father's mother, Ella Mae Fisher Fair. She loved us dearly and treated us well.. However, knowing that my biological mother never wanted me caused me to have extreme self-worth issues that led to severe depression. Back then, I wasn't able to identify it as depression. I truly did not know what was wrong with me. I just knew I was smiling on the outside, but on the inside, I felt worthless and unwanted.

That's one of the cruelest parts about depression: it's not always obvious to anyone else. You can still laugh. You can still get dressed. You can still post a picture. You can still take care of everybody. You can still "handle business." But inside, you feel hollow, like you're existing instead of living. Like something precious has been stolen from you and you don't even know when it happened or how to get it back. You may not even have the strength to explain it. Because depression doesn't come with neat sentences. It comes with fog and days of disorientation.

Depression can feel like guilt with no clear cause. Like shame that makes you second-guess your worth. It feels as if you're failing at life because you're not as "strong" as everyone thinks you should be. It can make the smallest tasks feel like climbing a mountain. Brushing your teeth or washing your face are no longer priorities. Returning a text is too much to ask and folding laundry is just out of the question. You can't seem to get in the shower or eat anything.. You have got brain fog and can't make a solid decision, and then you feel even worse because you're thinking, *"Why can't I just do it?"* Depression turns ordinary life into an exhausting dreaded performance.

I remember when I lived in Los Angeles California on 109th and Normandie. Although I was super young I had already been married and was separated by then from my first husband. He was a great provider but not as great at being a faithful husband. He also didn't mind throwing a punch at me from time to time. Nevertheless, I got married anyway at age 19, I was way too young to know how to navigate feelings or stand up for myself. I was still trying to work through my feelings of abandonment from my mother.

But let me tell you something that can help shift your entire healing process: depression is not your friend. It is not your identity. It's an enemy. It's a thief. It's a liar, and the first step to kicking anything in the butt is recognizing it for what it is, not what it claims you are. I felt If my own mother did not want me then no one would. That was a lie. When you are young and just trying to figure life out you believe the lies of the enemy. The enemy is that little voice in your head that makes you feel less than.

Depression is sneaky. It doesn't walk in and announce itself like, "Hello, I'm depression." and I will be here for two weeks. It comes disguised as "I'm just overwhelmed." Or "I'm just tired." Or "I'm just going through a lot." And yes, life can truly be heavy and overwhelming at times. However that is normal and something most human beings go through. They figure it out and find a solution to the problem and move forward. But when you are depressed you can not envision the solutions. You can not see the light.

Statistically, depression is far more common than most people realize. The World Health Organization estimates that **about 280 million people worldwide** live with depression, which is roughly **5% of adults**. World Health Organization+1 That means in almost every family, every neighborhood, every workplace, and every church, there are people smiling through something they can barely carry, and because depression is so often invisible, many suffer quietly for years, thinking they are the only one, thinking something is "wrong" with them, when really they are dealing with a real and widespread condition that deserves real support and real compassion.

And when depression is left untreated or ignored long enough, it can become deadly. The World Health Organization reports that **more than 720,000 people die by suicide every year worldwide**. World Health Organization In the United States alone, the CDC reports **over 49,000 deaths by suicide in 2023**, which is about **one death every 11 minutes**. That number is not just a statistic, it is someone's child, someone's parent, someone's friend, someone who laughed at the cookout, someone who showed up to work, someone who told everybody, "I'm fine," while privately fighting a war in their mind.

Depression can lead to death because it lies in a way that feels final. It slowly drains hope, then convinces you that hope is not coming back. It distorts your thinking until you start believing your pain is permanent and your life is the problem. It can isolate you from people who love you, silence you when you need to speak, and convince you that you are a burden when you are actually a blessing. That is how the danger grows, not always in one dramatic moment, but through a long season of feeling trapped, unseen, exhausted, and ashamed. Many people will never see the light, unfortunately, and that is heartbreaking. But that is also why I wrote this book, because I want you to know there is another ending available for your story, and you don't have to face this darkness alone.

If you or someone you love is ever in that dead-end place where suicide feels like an option, please reach for help immediately. In the United States, you can call or text **988** for the Suicide and Crisis Lifeline. If you are outside the U.S., your local emergency number or local crisis line can help you right away. You deserve support, you deserve safety, and you deserve the chance to live long enough to see that the lie was not the truth.

Spiritually, depression can feel like you're disconnected from everything good. Like your prayers bounce off the ceiling. It convinces you that you are not important enough for God to listen to you. It causes you to believe that God is far away, and you're the only one left in the room. It can feel like silence when you need comfort the most. That silence can mess with your mind because it makes you assume the worst: *"Maybe God forgot about me."* Or *"Maybe I'm being punished."* Or *"Maybe I'm not strong enough to be helped."* You will throw everything you did wrong in your own face and make that the reason God doesn't care. None of that Is true, but I understand getting you to the point where you accept and believe that you are a wonderful eternally loved creation of God that he has not abandoned will take some time. So hang in there with me because I have definitely been thee.

But I want to say this gently and clearly: your feelings are real, but they are not always telling the truth. There is a little voice in our head that speaks to us all day long, and when we are depressed, so much of what that voice says is distorted. It tells you you're not enough. It tells you you're alone. It tells you nothing will change. It tells you there's no point in trying, and the scary part is that it can sound like *you*, so you start believing it's truth when it's really just pain talking.

Stay hopeful, because that same inner voice can later feed you the complete opposite narrative. The mind that tells you "you'll never make it" can learn to say "I'm getting stronger." The voice that says "nobody cares" can learn to say "I am loved and supported." The voice that says "this will last forever" can learn to say "this is a season, and seasons change." Some people call that negative voice the devil when it's speaking darkness and defeat, and I understand why its hard to believe, because it tries to pull you away from hope, faith, and your future. But the most important thing I can tell you is this: you are not powerless against it. You are much stronger than you think. I am a living, breathing witness that it can all be turned around for the better.

Through daily positive tools, you can learn to switch that negative inner chatter to something that heals you instead of harms you. You can train your mind the same way you trained it to worry, to overthink, to be fearful, to doubt, and to expect disappointments in your life. You can interrupt the lies and replace them with truth. You can practice new thoughts until they become your new normal. Little by little, that voice that once tried to bury you can become a voice that builds you. Because your mind may be loud right now, but with consistency, support, and spiritual strength, you can teach it a new language, one that leads you back to peace.

There are seasons when your emotions will be louder than your faith. That doesn't mean you don't have faith. It means you're human. It means you've been carrying too much for too long. It means your soul is asking for love and care. Even the strongest people can break. Even the most faithful people can feel lost. Even the most "positive" people can have moments where the light goes dim. Depression doesn't mean you're weak, it means you're wounded, and wounds need attention, not judgment.

Recognizing the enemy also means telling the truth about what you've been through. Depression doesn't always come out of nowhere. Sometimes it's built from years of unspoken pain. Sometimes it's grief that never got processed. Sometimes it's childhood trauma you normalized because you had to survive it. Sometimes it's disappointment after disappointment until your hope gets tired. Sometimes it's betrayal. Sometimes it's rejection. Sometimes it's abuse. Sometimes it's simply the pressure of trying to be everything for everybody while nobody is checking on you. I tell my life coaching clients regularly "You Matter First." You must attend to your own mental , emotional, physical and spiritual need first. If you are weak in all of those areas, you will be no good for anyone else.

Yes, sometimes depression can come from chemical imbalance, hormone shifts, health issues, and stress overload. It's not always one reason. Depression can be layered. That's why you can't heal it by pretending it's not there. You can't out-smile it. You can't out-work it. You can't out-achieve it. At some point, you have to stop running from it and turn around and face it head on. Because what you don't confront will keep controlling you.

I used to go months and months happy as a lark. Then some life experience would happen and Bam! I'm depressed again. Life is going to keep presenting challenging experiences. We must learn to control how we react to them.

Here's what I want you to understand: you are not "crazy"

because you feel this way. You are not broken beyond repair. You are not too far gone. Depression is real, but so is recovery, and even if you can't feel it yet, there is still a part of you that wants to live and be happy. The fact that you opened this book proves that. The fact that you are still here means something. The fact that you are still searching means there is still light in you, even if it's small right now.

Sometimes the first victory is not a big celebration. Sometimes the first victory is simply saying, *"This is depression. This is not me."* Sometimes the first victory is admitting, *"I need help."* It's accepting that what has happened to you is not you. Sometimes the first victory is letting yourself cry without apologizing. Sometimes the first victory is telling the truth after years of holding it in. Sometimes the first victory is recognizing that you have been fighting a battle silently, and it's time to stop suffering in secret. We were not put on earth to suffer. The only person that can control how much you suffer is you.

Let's talk about what depression steals, because you need to know what you're fighting for. Depression steals your appetite for life. It steals your excitement. It steals your motivation. It steals your creativity. It steals your desire to connect. It steals your confidence. It steals your ability to imagine a better future. It can even steal your faith, not by removing God, but by blurring your vision so you can't *see* God through the fog. I absolutely blamed God for it all. Everything that happened in my life destroyed my faith in God. I'm so grateful I lived long enough to learn that God had already given me the tools I needed to get up everyday and feel magnificent about myself and my future.

God is not intimidated by your darkness. You don't have to get "better" before you come to Him. You can call on the Divine

Source from wherever you are. You don't have to clean yourself up to be worthy of comfort. Some of the strongest prayers you will ever pray won't be fancy. They'll be simple. They'll be raw. They'll sound like, *"God, I need You."* They'll sound like, *"Help me make it through today."* They'll sound like, *"Please hold me because I can't hold myself."* God is a unseen Divine spiritual force that created us all, who is always working in your favor. God is not a old wise man in the heaven waiting to judge you. He created you with the power to design a beautiful life for yourself. I want you to think of God as a powerful, positive energy that loves you, and think of the Devil as a powerful unseen energy that hates you. The key is understanding that you have the ultimate control over which one of these energies you give in to.

Recognizing the enemy also means recognizing the patterns. Depression has habits. It isolates you. It convinces you to cancel plans and makes you avoid friends and family. You stop picking up phone calls. It makes you feel like a burden. It makes you feel like nobody understands. It makes you replay old mistakes like a movie that never ends. It makes you romanticize disappearing, not necessarily physically, but emotionally. You stop showing up as yourself. You become a shadow of who you were. The longer it goes unrecognized, the more "normal" it starts to feel. You start to accept it as your baseline.

But we are not accepting depression as your baseline. We are not making peace with something that is trying to destroy your livelihood and your peace of mind. We are not calling this "Just life" when it's actually a battle for your mind, your heart, and your future.

Depression is what Joyce Meyers called the "Battlefield of the Mind" and Mind is all. I have a little motivational slogan I created about the mind.

MIND: **M** = Manipulating Ideas **I**=In a **N**=New **D**=Direction

This chapter is your line in the sand, it will teach you to manipulate your inner and outer speech in a direction that serves you best. You will learn tools that assist in turning that darkness into beautiful light. I am speaking from experience. I have survived many different episodes of extreme depression.

This book will help you say: *"I see you, depression. I know what you are. You've been hiding in my tiredness, my numbness, my silence, my irritability, my procrastination, my over-eating, my under-eating, my sleepless nights, my panic, my self deprecating language, my shame, my lack of motivation, my social withdrawal, my constant "I'm fine." But I recognize you now and I challenge you to a fight.*

Once you recognize the enemy, that dark invasive energy, you can stop blaming yourself for being under attack. You can find tools and daily practices that help you fight for your life. You can stop calling yourself lazy when you're actually drained. You can stop calling yourself weak when you've actually been fighting. You can stop calling yourself "too much" when you've actually been carrying too much. You can begin to separate who you are from what you're experiencing and that separation is powerful.

You are not depression. You are not your worst day or your darkest thought. We all have dark thoughts at times. You are not your emptiest moment. What has happened to you is not you. You are not what you may have done to yourself. You are not what you lost. You are not what you fear. You are a phenomenal creation of God with limitless potential.

You are still you, under those covers, under the heaviness in that dark room you don't want to come out of. I believe with everything in me that the real you is still in there, waiting to breathe again. Waiting to remember how great you are. So it's time to get up and start "Kicking Depression in the Butt." Does not matter if you are a man, woman or child. Get up Now! So as we begin this journey.

I want you to promise yourself something: you will not minimize or attempt to numb your pain, you will allow yourself to feel with the knowing that It will pass and you have control over when it does. You will also not surrender your future. You will stop pretending. You will stop suffering alone. You will start telling the truth about your feeling so that you can begin to heal them. You will start learning and implementing tools that make you feel better. You will start rebuilding your mind. You will start reclaiming your spirit. You will start creating a life that supports your healing, not just a life that looks good to other people.

Because you deserve to feel light again. You deserve to feel hopeful again.

You deserve to enjoy your life again because Life is Beautiful. Depression doesn't get to have the final word. **Not** this time. **Not** with you. **Not** while you're reading this. **Not** while your spirit is still fighting to come back to the surface.

This is the beginning of your transformation and I'm beyond excited for you. Please remember that **You are Great and this is your Life to Create, So Lets Go!**

2

Breaking The Thought Cycle

Depression doesn't just sit on your chest, it talks and narrates stores that are not always true. It comments on everything you do and everything you don't do. It turns your mind into a courtroom where you're always the one on trial, always the one being questioned, always the one being found guilty. If you don't recognize that voice for what it is, you'll start treating its opinions like facts. You'll start believing that your worst thoughts are the truest version of you. But they're not. They are symptoms and learned patterns. Great thing is, those patterns can be interrupted.

Whether you accept it or not, you taught yourself how to belittle and disrespect you. You led the charge on the only attacks against you that truly matter, because the attacks from the outside world are far less damaging than the ones you do to yourself. There is an old African proverb that says, "If there is no enemy on the inside, the enemy on the outside can do you no harm." When I speak motivationally, I always introduce this quote to the audience. It is so very powerful if you allow it to sink in. There is no damage greater than the self-inflicted pain we cause ourselves. The internal enemy does more damage than any outside enemy ever could. We can be our own worst enemy, the masters of self- sabotage.

For example, no one ever walked up to me and reminded me that I was an abandoned child. I did that. I told myself repeatedly that I was not worthy because my own mother did not want me. I now know that was a lie. Her drug addiction and the choices she made during it had nothing to do with me. But choosing to take it personally caused me over forty years of pain. This book was written to help you avoid that.

That is exactly how a thought cycle works. A thought cycle is not just "thinking negative." It's repetitive. It's the same sentence in different outfits. It's the same fear wearing different faces. Your mind automatically reaching for the worst-case scenario because somewhere along the way, pain trained you to expect pain. It's waking up and already feeling defeated before you even get out of bed. It's remembering one mistake and using it as evidence that *you* are a mistake. It's replaying a conversation from five years ago like it happened this morning. It's looking in the mirror and hearing criticism instead of compassion. Depression loves cycles because cycles keep you stuck. When you're stuck, you don't move, and when you don't move, you don't change. When there is no change, depression feels safe and hangs around for much longer. This applies to the strongest of men and even innocent children, Depression does not just strike woman. Anyone can experience it.

The reason this matters so much is because depression doesn't always start with what people do to you; sometimes it deepens because of what you keep saying to youself. It's the private narrative you repeat when nobody else is around. It's the labels you place on yourself. It's the meaning you attach

13

to what happened to you. It's the way you interpret rejection, disappointment, delay, and pain. When you repeatedly agree with the worst interpretation, your mind starts building a home there. It becomes familiar. It becomes your default. Then you don't even realize you're living under attack, because you have called the attack "truth."

Unfortunately, I witnessed a tragic murder at a very young age. My beloved grandmother was killed right in front of me by her husband of thirty-two years. I lived with them after my own mother tried to kill me as a three-month-old baby by putting me into a suitcase and closing it. My grandmother was amazing. She was a old school county woman from Dallas, Texas. She raised me and my older sister as her own, and she loved us dearly. When I was seventeen years old, my grandfather shot her in the head in front of me.

That was the day my life changed. That is the day that I lost all hope in God and humanity. I'm sure this indecent was the source, along with the maternal abandonment, of my early onset of depression. I suffered for many years with PTSD, which is **Post-Traumatic Stress Disorder**, and depression. I did not begin the journey of healing until my late thirties because I did not know I could heal from something that horrendous. But I did, and you can too. It was far from easy but I want you to know that healing is possible.

Because the moment you recognize the enemy on the inside, you also recognize your power to cast that enemy out. If your words helped create the prison, your words can also help build the exit. If your mind learned to repeat the lie or negative memory, your mind can also be trained to repeat the truth.

The truth is, there is light on the other side of darkness. You can and you will feel better one day. But the work is not just about "feeling better," it's about thinking better on purpose. It's about catching the sentence before it becomes a cycle. It's about interrupting the old story before it talks you out of your future. It is about choosing not to replay that past trauma or tragedy over and over in your head. It's about finally giving yourself what you should have been giving yourself all along: compassion, understanding, grace, and a new narrative that leads you toward healing instead of keeping you stuck in the pain of the past.

Your mind was never meant to trap you in darkness. It has the capacity to grow, create, and restore, much like a garden that responds to the care it receives. Anyone who has planted something understands that growth does not happen by accident. Attention matters. What you consistently nurture begins to take root, and what you neglect does not simply disappear; it either withers or becomes tangled and overgrown. Depression can take hold in that same quiet way. It builds slowly in the unspoken thoughts, in the shame that goes unaddressed, in the exhaustion that never gets resolved, and in the isolation that convinces you to withdraw even further. Over time it can feel as though everything inside you has been overtaken. That feeling does not mean you are broken beyond repair. Nor does it mean your inner world is ruined. It means care has been delayed. It means support and new habits are needed. Healing requires intention, just as tending a garden requires patience and the right tools. With steady effort, healthier thoughts can be planted, destructive patterns can be pulled out at the root, and light can reach places that once felt permanently shaded. Nothing about your mind is beyond renewal, but it does require participation.

Breaking the thought cycle begins with one brave moment

of honesty. You have to catch the thought in the act. I call it *"Catch and Cast." I have a few videos on YouTube and a book on online with that title. Catch and Cast. C*atch that negative thought and cast it right on out of your head. then replace it with a new empowering, uplifting thought. A Thought that makes you feel great about yourself. Catch it quickly not after it's already dragged you into a horrible mood. Do not wait until it has already ruined your whole day. Not after you've already spiraled into the "what's the point" place. You have to learn to notice the moment the narrative starts. Depression usually begins with a simple sentence. "I'm tired." "I can't do this." "Nobody cares about me." "Nothing ever changes." "What's wrong with me?" These sentences sound normal because they're familiar. Familiar doesn't mean true. Familiar just means rehearsed. It is something that you have done repeatedly. It means something is already embedded into your subconscious.

The enemy that prevents healing is automatic thinking. Automatic thinking is when your mind responds before you even ask it to. Something goes wrong, and immediately your mind says, "Of course." Someone doesn't call back, and immediately your mind says, "See, nobody wants me" You wake up heavy, and immediately your mind says, "Today is going to be terrible." That's the cycle. It's not just the thought. It's the speed of the thought. The thought arrives like it owns the place, and you accept it like it pays rent. But the truth is, you don't have to agree with every thought that visits you.

There is power in simply pausing, and taking a deep breath. It's a spiritual kind of power. A holy kind of power. A positive tool we all should use. Because a pause gives you space to breathe, and a breathing gives you space to think and choose your response. Depression wants you to react. It wants you to accept. It wants you to surrender. But when you pause, you disrupt the pattern. You begin to take your authority back. You begin to say, "Wait a minute. That is a thought. That is not a prophecy. That is a feeling. That is not my future. That is a memory. That is not my identity." You can then make a conscious choice to cast the negativity right on out of there.

A lot of people assume that having faith means you never struggle with dark or negative thoughts. That idea has caused more shame than healing. Faith is not the absence of mental battles. It is how you respond when those battles begin. Thoughts will come. Feelings will rise. Some days your mind may feel louder than your peace. The measure of faith is not whether negativity appears; it is whether you decide to let it define you.

When heavy thoughts surface, that is where faith becomes active. It is the moment you pause and choose which voice you are going to listen to and agree with. Depression may whisper that you are alone, forgotten, or incapable, but faith reminds you that feelings are not final truth. Faith is the quiet but firm decision to believe that God's presence remains steady even when your emotions fluctuate. It is the willingness to say, even through tears, that you are not abandoned just because you feel low. It is the courage to recognize that your thoughts are loud, but they are not in charge.

Choosing faith means refusing to let every thought take the driver's seat. It means understanding that your mind can produce noise without producing truth. You can experience sadness without becoming sadness. You can feel discouraged without surrendering your identity to discouragement. Faith steps in and says that your current emotion does not get to write your entire story. It anchors you in something deeper than your mood.

This is where the work begins. The tools you will learn are not meant for perfect days; they are meant for the hard ones. Faith becomes a daily practice of alignment, a conscious return to what is steady when everything inside feels unstable. It is not pretending you are fine. It is remembering who you are and who God is, even when your mind tries to convince you otherwise.

Depression tries to make you speak against yourself. It tries to make you curse your future with your mouth. It tries to make you describe your life in a way that keeps you trapped. It wants you to say, "I'll never be happy." "I'll never be normal." "I'll never heal." And when you repeat those sentences, your spirit begins to memorize them. Your body begins to respond to them. Your choices begin to follow them. Words are not just sounds. Words are seeds. One of the most life-changing decisions you can make is to stop planting seeds that grow more darkness. You are the gardener of your life. You must decide what you will plant.

Breaking the thought cycle is not pretending everything is fine. It's telling the truth with power. It's saying, "This is hard, but it is not hopeless." It's saying, "I feel heavy, but I am still moving." It's saying, "I'm struggling today, but I will not quit on myself." It's saying, "I'm not where I want to be, but I am not where I used to be." It's giving your mind a new sentence to repeat. Not a fake sentence. A strengthening sentence. A sentence with backbone. A sentence with spirit. A sentence that represents your understanding that there is a universal law of Eb and Flow. Bad times will not last forever. God designed everything to have a season. Depression is a season that will pass.

I teach my children to record positive affirmations on their cell phones and drift off to sleep while listening to them. That is a tool I used to implant the positive thoughts into my subconscious mind. It works.

You have to understand this about your brain: repetition creates grooves. The more you think a thought, the easier it becomes to think that thought again. You can choose to stop thinking a specific thought. Find uplifting things that distract you. Create positive habitual habits and eventually they will become second nature.

Depression feels like it has momentum. It does because you have been doing it consistently for years sometimes. It has been practiced. It has been accepted as belief. But the same rule works for healing. The more you practice a new thought, the more natural it becomes. The more you speak life, the more your mind starts to recognize life. The more you choose self-compassion, the more your nervous system begins to calm. This is not just motivational talk. This is how your mind is wired. Depression did not become strong overnight, and healing does not become strong overnight. But it does become strong.

There will be days when the thought cycle feels like a wave you can't stop. On those days, your goal is not to win with perfection. Your goal is to win with interruption. Even if you only interrupt the cycle for a minute, that minute matters. Even if all you can say is, "Not today Satan" Even if all you can do is breathe and whisper, "God help me." Even if all you can manage is to get out of bed and sit up. Interruption is a victory. It is proof that you are still in the fight. As long as you have breath in your body the fight is not over. Each day you awake you are presented with a new opportunity to *"Kick Depression in the Butt"*

Depression loves isolation because isolation gives it a microphone. When you're alone too long, your thoughts get louder. Your fear gets creative. Your shame gets persuasive. So part of breaking the cycle is refusing to disappear. It's choosing connection even when you don't feel like talking. It's letting one safe person know you're not okay. It's refusing to pretend. It's allowing support to touch you. It letting that supportive family member hug you. Because healing is not just personal, it is relational. Even when depression says, "Stay away," you have to remember that love is medicine.

And listen, there is nothing wrong with getting professional help. There is nothing un-spiritual about therapy. I had many therapist when I was suffering with depression. There is nothing weak about medication if you need it. God works through people. God works through wisdom. God works through tools. Sometimes healing is prayer and breath. Sometimes healing is prayer and boundaries. Sometimes healing is prayer and a counselor. Sometimes healing is prayer and learning how to sleep again or laugh again. You do not have to choose between faith and help. You can hold both. You can be spiritual and still need support. You can love God and still need a practical plan.

Breaking the thought cycle also means forgiving yourself for having the cycle in the first place. Some of you feel guilty for being depressed, and that guilt becomes another layer of pain. You feel bad for feeling bad. You criticize yourself for struggling. You compare your private battle to someone else's public smile. That is not healing. That is self-harm in a polite outfit. You deserve tenderness. You deserve patience. You deserve compassion. The same grace you give everyone else is the grace you must learn to give yourself. You come first. You can not be of help or service to anyone if you are suffering.

I named my first book **My Spiritual Smile** for a reason. At the time, I was running a successful business in Los Angeles called **Braids By SaBrina**, and I had several young women from similar backgrounds working for me. I was also raising children alone, so I learned how to keep going no matter what. I became the kind of woman who could handle business, take care of everybody, and still show up with a smile. I was always smiling on the outside. But on the inside, I was broken. My inner joy, my spiritual smile I would not find until much later in life.

I had suppressed witnessing the murder of my grandmother. I never spoke about it in the first ten years after it happened, and I carried that silence like it was normal. I got married young and lived my life as if nothing had ever happened to me, as if I could just keep moving forward and outpace the pain. I tried to live like the past didn't exist, like trauma could be buried and never resurface. But trauma doesn't disappear just because you don't talk about it. It waits and hides, and as time went on, everything I had suppressed began to surface as anger.

I can't go back and do things differently, but I can choose what I do with my story now. If this book can help others deal with their trauma and hurt differently, then I have done my job. No matter who you are or what you have been through, you can heal, and you do not have to carry that pain with you for life. You deserve to live a happy, fulfilling life.

Here is what I want you to hold close as you move through this chapter and beyond it: you are not powerless in your own mind. You may not control the first thought that pops up, but you can control the thought you partner with. You may not be able to stop every wave, but you can learn how to surf. You may not be able to erase the past, but you can stop rehearsing it until it becomes your whole identity. You can decide that your mind will no longer be a place where you get attacked all day.

You are learning to interrupt the lie. You are learning to replace the script. You are learning to speak to yourself like someone you love. You are learning to choose life in small, consistent moments. Those moments are how you win your battle with depression.

Because one day you will look back and realize the cycle broke, not because you had one perfect day, but because you had a thousand small interruptions. You had a thousand moments where you chose a better sentence, where you caught and cast out the negative thought. You had a thousand moments where you refused to agree with the darkness. You had a thousand moments where you kept showing up for yourself. That is how depression gets kicked in the butt.

3

Smiling While You're Suffering

There is a special kind of pain that comes from being the one everyone thinks is okay, and that has always been me. I was the owner of **Braids By SaBrina** for over twenty-six years, and I always had younger women working for me who looked to me for leadership. Most of them had no idea about the tragedies I had been through. I wasn't intentionally hiding anything; I had simply buried that pain so far down that sometimes I forgot it was even there. I was the consistent one who showed up daily, opened the door for my staff, and provided them a place to make a living. I was the leader, the one who kept it together. The one who still took care of business, still cracked jokes, still posted pictures, and still said, "I'm good."

Meanwhile, I was quietly falling apart on the inside. I was smiling with tears behind my eyes. I was laughing while my chest felt tight. I was being strong because I did not feel like I had permission to be anything else. After a while, that kind of strength starts to feel like a prison. When pain is buried long enough, it doesn't disappear, it builds pressure, eventually, it will erupt like a volcano and spill out into your life.

Many people have no idea how draining it is to keep pretending everything is fine. A smile can be convincing. Productivity can look like progress. Simply showing up every day can give the impression that healing has already happened. What often goes unseen is the weight being carried underneath all of that performance. Depression does not always remove you from your responsibilities; sometimes it teaches you how to function while quietly unraveling inside. You can be present in the room, answering questions, meeting deadlines, taking care of everyone else, yet feel emotionally distant from your own life. From the outside, everything appears steady. Internally, it feels heavy and disconnected. That silent split is where so many people live for years without anyone realizing how much they are struggling.

Pretending usually begins as self protection. At some point, you learned that pushing through was safer than falling apart. Reliability became your shield. You figured out how to wipe your tears, fix your face, and reenter a room as though nothing had happened. That ability helped you survive difficult seasons. It kept things moving. It earned you praise for being strong. Over time, however, survival strategies can turn into permanent patterns. The performance becomes automatic. You grow so skilled at appearing okay that you lose touch with what honesty feels like. When someone asks how you are, the polished answer comes out before you even check in with yourself.

Living that way is exhausting because it separates you from your own truth. Healing cannot begin where pretending continues. In this book, I am going to walk you through the process that helped me stop performing and start confronting what was really happening inside. Prayer matters. Faith matters. At the same time, change requires participation. Peace does not appear simply because we hope for it; it grows when we decide to do the work that supports it. Fighting for your happiness is not selfish. It is necessary. You deserve more than survival. You deserve to feel fully alive in your own life.

I remember the few times, as a young woman, that I actually let it all out. I cried, and I told someone about the abandonment and abuse from my mother, and about the murder of my grandmother. At first, they seemed loving and compassionate, like they were truly listening. But by the time I got to the end of the story, the look on their face registered to me as, "Wow... that's a big one. I don't know if I can help you with that." It crushed me.

No one knew how to tell a young woman who watched her grandmother's head blown off by her grandfather that everything was going to be okay, and it showed in their eyes. It felt like they quietly wrote me off as permanently broken. Because I could see and feel that distance in them, I retreated even farther inside, vowing never to speak of those things again. It hurt me, and it taught me that sharing my past was not a safe space.

After that, I started editing myself before I even opened my mouth. I learned how to tell the "acceptable" version of my story, the one that didn't make people uncomfortable, the one that didn't change the energy in the room. I learned how to keep the hardest parts locked away behind a smile, because it felt safer to carry the pain alone than to watch someone's face shift again. I didn't want pity. I didn't want someone to fix me. I just wanted to be heard without feeling like my truth was too heavy to hold. But when you don't have language for trauma, and the people around you don't have understanding for it either, silence starts to feel like the only option.

The more I stayed silent, the more isolated I became on the

inside. I could be surrounded by people and still feel completely alone, because no one was meeting the real me, only the version of me I served them. I had given up on healing. I lived with the nightmare of the murder and figured I would forever. I became skilled at surviving, but I didn't know how to be safe. I became skilled at functioning, but I didn't know how to be free. That kind of loneliness is its own kind of pain, because it convinces you that if people really knew what you carried, they would step back. It makes you believe that your story disqualifies you from love, from peace, from joy. That is exactly how trauma deepens, when you start carrying it not only as a memory, but as a secret.

Because of the tragedy, and because I was out in the world at a young age trying to navigate life with more pain than guidance, I got married at nineteen to my 12th-grade boyfriend. He was older than me and a great provider, and the truth is, I didn't have anywhere else to go. My older sister was away at college in San Diego. Our father had died when we were ten and eleven. Our mother was still out in the world, addicted to drugs. We had lost the one stable home we had ever known, the home filled with love and security with our grandparents, when our grandfather killed our grandmother.

At the time, I believed I loved my first husband. But what does a nineteen-year-old with PTSD and abandonment issues truly know about love? When you've lived through trauma, love can start to feel like safety, and safety can start to feel like rescue. Sometimes you don't choose marriage because you're ready; sometimes you choose it because you're trying to survive. Sometimes you aren't looking for a partner as much as you're looking for a place to land. I was looking for somewhere, anywhere, that didn't feel like loss.

So in August of 1989, I married **Clyde Arnold Reece**. my first

26

child an dour only son Justin Clyde Reece was born a few months earlier on February 18, 1989. I carried into that marriage not just a dream for a better life, but also a whole history of grief, fear, and survival that I didn't yet have the words to explain. I was trying to build a future while still bleeding from the past, and I didn't know then what I know now: unhealed pain doesn't disappear just because you put on a wedding dress.

There is a deeper layer that many people do not talk about. Smiling while suffering can become a way of avoiding what you really feel. Because if you slow down, you might have to face the grief you buried. If you stop moving, you might have to admit you are lonely. If you tell the truth, you might have to accept that you are tired of holding everything together. Sometimes the smile is not just for others. Sometimes it is for you. Sometimes it is the cover you put over your own pain so you do not have to look at it.

But your soul knows. Your body and your spirit know. Eventually, the weight shows up somewhere. It shows up in anxiety. It shows up in extreme erratic behavior, It shows up in irritable sleepless nights. It shows up in exhaustion that rest does not fix. For some it shows up in losing motivation, in feeling numb. The moments when you are alone and the mask finally slips, and you realize you have been holding your breath emotionally for a long time.

Spiritually, this chapter matters because depression loves hidden places. It thrives in secrecy. It grows in silence. It gets stronger when you feel like you have to protect everyone else from the truth of what you are going through. But healing happens in the light. It happens when you stop trying to look strong and start allowing yourself to get supported by the ones who love you. Healing happens when you admit, even to God,

27

that you are not okay. Not as a dramatic statement, but as an honest one. Because God cannot heal what you keep denying. God cannot comfort the version of you that is always pretending. God meets you in truth. Truth and acknowledgment is the first step towards a better life. I tell my kids all the time.

I will never be depressed again. That can become truth for you as well. Not because life will stop presenting challenges. But because you will now have the tools as I did, the tools to drag yourself up and out of that bed and take charge of your own future. You will have the daily practical tools to uplift and encourage yourself.

Some of you have been using faith as another mask. You have been saying the right spiritual words while your heart is breaking. You go around quoting scriptures while your mind is spiraling. You tell everyone to trust God while, privately, you feel abandoned by God. You feel like you are not allowed to struggle because you love God. But faith is not the absence of pain. Faith is what you cling to while you are in pain. There is nothing wrong with saying, "God, I love You, but I am hurting." "God, I believe, but I am tired." "God, I know You are real, but I do not feel You right now." That is not weak. That is real and honest, and that is where healing begins.

God has already instilled the help you need inside of you. Faith without works is dead. You must get up and stop looking to the sky, waiting for the heavens to open and for God to descend and give you the answers. You have them already, inside of you. The Kingdom of Heaven is inside of you already. You have to initiate the healing and stop depending on the pastor or the therapist to do it for you.

Get up right now, whether you are a man, woman, or child. Walk over to the mirror and look at yourself. Take a deep, long breath. Say, "I am ready, now." "No more suffering for me." "I am healed and happy, from this day forward." Speak it with emotion, passion, and certainty, and as sure as my name is **SaBrina Fisher Romania Reece**, it will become your reality. Speak it now. Live it later. Do not give up.

Make this a daily ritual, speaking as if the healing has already taken place. Let it apply to your mental, physical, emotional, financial, and spiritual healing.

It's ok to smile outwardly while doing the work needed inwardly. Smiling while suffering is also connected to the role you play in other people's lives. Maybe you are the strong one in your family. Maybe you are the helper. The provider. The one people call when they need advice. The one who is always there. When you are that person, it can feel like you are not allowed to fall apart. You might think, If I break, everything breaks. So you keep going. You keep carrying. You keep showing up. But you were never meant to carry everybody and carry yourself through depression at the same time. That is too much for any human being. Keep Smiling because that invites a positive healing energy into your life but make sure you are actively doing the work needed to smile from the inside as well.

There is a difference between being strong and being silent. There is a difference between being private and being trapped. You do not owe the whole world your story, but you do owe yourself honesty. You deserve to have at least one safe space where you can productively release. You deserve to have at least one person who can hold the truth without judging you. You deserve to have a moment where you are not performing, where you are not explaining, where you are not pretending, where you can simply be.

Stop viewing crying a negative. Change your perception and

view every tear as a release of pain, toxins and stress from your life.

One of the biggest lies depression tells is that you are a burden. It tells you that if you speak up, you will annoy people. It tells you that if you admit you are struggling, you will disappoint others. It tells you that your pain makes you too much. But the truth is, the people who truly love you would rather know how they can help you, than to lose you. The people who truly care would rather hear the truth than keep clapping for a performance that is draining your life. Even if some people do not understand, that does not mean your truth is wrong. It just means they are not equipped. Please do not take that personally. Give them a hug and move forward.

This chapter is your permission slip to stop pretending. Not because you are giving up, but because you are ready to heal. You are allowed to tell the truth. You are allowed to rest. You are allowed to cry. You are allowed to ask for help. You are allowed to say, "I have been smiling, but I have been suffering." You are allowed to say, "I need support." You are allowed to say, "I am tired of being strong alone." Healing does not require you to perform, and it does not require you to suffer in silence. It requires honesty, and it requires courage.

And I also want to be responsible and clear about something important. If you have been prescribed medication, take the medication you are prescribed. If you are under the care of a doctor or therapist, follow their guidance and their treatment plan. Keep your appointments. Ask questions. Be honest about how you are feeling. Get professional help when you need it, and do not stop medication suddenly or change your dosage without talking to your doctor. There is no shame in using medical support as a part of your healing. There is wisdom in it.

But at the same time, I want you to understand that medication and therapy are not meant to replace you, they are meant to support you. They can help stabilize you, guide you, and give you tools, but the key to full healing still involves your participation. Combined with medical care, you must do the internal work yourself. You must take ownership of your thoughts, your habits, your boundaries, and the way you speak to yourself when no one else is around. You have to choose healing daily, not just when you feel strong, but especially when you feel tired.

That is why I am so serious about mindset. That is why I'm encouraging you to speak your affirmations daily. I realize they may feel like untruths at first, especially if you've been living in pain for a long time. But trust me, eventually they will not. You are not speaking affirmations to ignore reality; you are speaking them to interrupt the lies depression repeats and to train your mind to come into agreement with hope. Over time, your mindset will shift. You will begin to think differently, respond differently, and live differently, more happy, more hopeful, and more free.

And let this be the balance you carry forward: do the professional work and do the personal work. Let your doctor help you. Let your therapist guide you. Let medication, when needed, support your brain and body. But also show up for your own healing with consistency and intention. Because nobody can live your life for you. Nobody can make your daily choices for you. When you combine medical support with personal responsibility, you stop waiting to be rescued and you start rebuilding, one truth, one tool, one day at a time.

There is something powerful that happens when you stop performing happiness. You make room for real peace. Not the kind of peace that comes from everything going perfectly, but the kind of peace that comes from being honest, being supported, and being held. Real peace begins when you stop abandoning yourself to please everybody else. Real peace begins when you stop making your pain invisible.

You do not have to wear the mask forever. You do not have to keep proving you are okay. You do not have to be the strong one every day. You can be human. You can be in the process of healing. You can be honest and you can still be powerful, happy and peaceful.

Because the strongest people are not the ones who never struggle. The strongest people are the ones who stop pretending and start recovering on purpose. The strongest people are the ones who decide they deserve a life that feels good on the inside, not just a life that looks good on the outside.

4

Triggers, Trauma, and Holes: Finding the Root

Depression rarely shows up as a random visitor. Sometimes it does, but more often it arrives carrying history. It arrives with receipts. It arrives with memories your mind tried to pack away so you could keep functioning. It arrives with old pain that never got a safe place to land. This is why healing is not just about "feeling better." Healing is about telling the truth and finding the root cause. Not the polite truth. Not the version that keeps everybody comfortable. The truth that explains why your body reacts the way it reacts, why your heart shuts down, why your mind spirals, why certain situations make you feel like you are back in a place you promised yourself you would never return to.

Unfortunately, in many families there are secrets. It does not matter the nationality or economic status. Those old, buried secrets are still causing someone, right now, to not live up to their full potential in life. I'm in no way suggesting having hurtful, explosive conversations with family that most likely won't prove to be fruitful anyway. I'm suggesting having those conversations with yourself. Digging deep within. Who are you mad at? Who hurt you? Who violated you? Who devalued you? You must identify the root so you can kill it.

For years, I waited on my mother to find me and tell me that she loved me, and that she was so sorry. I waited eagerly, believing that she held the key to my happiness, but she never came. When I finally gathered the courage to go to her, hoping she would fix me, I realized she was incapable of doing so.

I will never forget the day I walked up the cement walkway to her apartment. I was 45 years old. The sun was beaming down on my face, and my heart was pounding so hard in my chest. I reached the front door and lightly knocked, but no one answered. I knocked a second time, and a faint voice said, "Who is it?" I nervously replied, "It's me. It's SaBrina, your daughter."

One of my younger sisters opened the door and let me inside. My mother, who had in recent years gone blind, sat on a couch in the living room. My sister pulled up a chair for me near my mother, and then she sat across from the both of us. My younger sister then turned to me and warned me to stay calm. The me that she remembered was filled with anger and rage for our mother.

I anticipated that this would be a long, emotional conversation, and I didn't want to forget the details, so I brought a small tape recorder.

I turned the recorder on and began to ask my mother a series of questions: "How did you meet my father?" "Who introduced you to drugs?" "Were you abused as a child?" "How could you abandon and abuse six children?" "Did your parents love you?"

Finally, I asked the most important question of all: "Did you really put me into a suitcase as a three-month-old baby with the intent to take my life?"

34

I sat there in silence, eagerly awaiting an answer. I knew that this would be the day I had been dreaming of for years. I just knew that she would cry and embrace me and tell me no, she would never do that, and that I had been lied to all these years. I waited for her to say that she was sorry for not being there, and for allowing drugs to cause her to leave and hurt all six of her children.

Instead, she looked in my direction and said, "Yes. Yes, I did put you into a suitcase because you cried too damn much as a baby."

My heart sank. Time seemed to stand still. I could not believe what I was hearing. Although I had already been told the story and hated her for it, I just knew that she would tell me it wasn't true and give me what I would serve as an acceptable response to my question, a response that would make me finally feel whole, a response that would make it easy for me to understand her actions. That was not the case. My heart broke, and in that moment, the pain seemed unbearable. I took a deep breath and looked directly at her, and I said something I never imagined I would say to her: "I forgive you."

Something that I can't fully explain, some force, in that moment, gave me the comfort and the knowledge that I was sent there for myself and not for her. No sooner than the pain of her response hit, something else, which I call the "Divine source of love, God" made me instantly realize that I was sent there to release the pain and resentment I'd held for her, because it was preventing me from fully loving myself. I realized that her actions had nothing to do with me. I had no control over if or when she would ever deal with and rectify her behavior. I knew then that from that day forward, I could not depend on her to make me feel loved and worthy of life. It was up to me, and holding on to the anger and pain was preventing me from returning to my true, God-given nature of love. Human beings can not heal you.

When I walked out of that apartment, it felt like I was seeing the beauty of the world for the very first time. Not because she gave me hugs and tears of love and regret or gave me all the answers I needed. But because I now understood why I was so compelled to go, and that God needed me to understand and take charge of my role in my own healing.

As I was leaving I glanced at the grass, which seemed to be a brighter green. I looked up at the sky, and it seemed to be a beautiful, radiant blue that I had never noticed before. It's apparent to me now that making the choice to forgive my mother, despite her never having said the long-awaited words that I expected her to say, was the only true way for me to grow. Even though she never begged for my forgiveness, embraced me, or showered me with the love I thought I could not survive without, forgiveness changed my life. Making the choice to forgive her, even though she never asked, was not easy, but in that moment I knew it was what I had to do for me. I decided that day that even if I never saw her again, I had forgiven her and was finally ready to move forward and learn to truly love myself, which was one of the best decisions I have ever made. It is what I want for each and every one of you. That weight can finally be lifted and you can experience a wonderful life.

The thought of my mother was always a trigger for me. Her very name always brought me to tears and extreme anger. A trigger is not weakness. A trigger is evidence. It is your nervous system remembering what your mouth may not say out loud. It is your brain recognizing danger based on past experiences, even when the danger is no longer in the room. Triggers can be obvious, like a specific place, a smell, a tone of voice, a holiday, a song, a certain time of year. But triggers can also be quiet and confusing. It can be someone not texting back or a change in someone's energy. It can be conflict or feeling ignored. It can be being criticized. It can even be love, because love can feel unsafe when you have known abandonment. It can also be success, because success sometimes reminds you of who never clapped for you.

I have definitely dealt with being super successful and still feeling hurt when others did not clap for me. It's normal to expect the ones who say they love you to celebrate you, to speak the words of congratulations, to show up with support, but they do not always say them. They do not always show up for you. That is why you must learn to congratulate yourself. I have written twelve or more self-help books, spoken motivationally as the keynote speaker at over 40 events, sustained a business where I employed over 1700 women for 30 years and when I post any of my accomplishments online hoping for support, I get crickets, especially from the people closest to me. I laugh at it now, but it can still be hurtful. What's interesting is that if I post something that makes people think I'm in distress, just from the dramatic title I chose , Wah-La!, all of a sudden there are hundreds of responses. I don't have time to figure out why the world sometimes prefers trauma over triumph, or negative over positive, but I do know this: it can be disappointing, and it can trigger those old self-worth feelings to rise up again. Don't let it. Don't let the silence of others talk you out of your confidence. Don't let a lack of applause make you question your value.

Because when you are triggered, the emotion you feel in the moment is often bigger than the moment itself. That's how you know something deeper is underneath it. You are not "overreacting", you are reacting to layers. You are reacting to old grief, old fear, old rejection, old humiliation, old pain. You are reacting to the parts of you that learned to protect themselves by staying on guard. Your mind and body have been trying to keep you safe the best way they know how. Sometimes that protection looks like anger. Sometimes it looks like shutting down. Sometimes it looks like needing control. Sometimes it looks like people pleasing. Sometimes it looks like perfectionism. Sometimes it looks like numbness. Sometimes it looks like depression.

Trauma is not just what happened. Trauma is what happened inside you because of what happened to you. It is the wound you carry after the event is over. It is the way your body learned to brace itself. It is the way your heart learned to expect disappointment. It is the way your mind learned to prepare for the next blow. Trauma can come from big events, like abuse, violence, loss, betrayal, accidents, neglect. But trauma can also come from repeated emotional experiences that taught you the same painful message over and over. Being dismissed and unheard. Being criticized or shamed. Being compared. Being chosen last. Being loved inconsistently. Being forced to grow up too fast. Being treated like your feelings were an inconvenience.

Sometimes the root is not one moment. Sometimes the root is a long season in your life. Possibly a season where you were surviving, and you did not have time to feel true emotions. A season where you kept going because you had to, and now your body is collecting the debt. Depression can be that debt. It can be what shows up when the adrenaline wears off, or what happens after you have been strong for too long. It can be your soul finally saying, I cannot keep doing this without care. Stop and fuel your own mind, body and spirit before you move forward in life. fill up your own cup because you matter most.

Finding the root is not about blaming others the past. It is about understanding yourself. Learning to have compassion for yourself. It is about gaining the wisdom needed to heal and prosper. if you do not know where the pain started, you will keep trying to treat symptoms while the wound stays open. You will keep trying to "think positive" while your nervous system is still living in survival mode. You will pray away what requires healing, support, and tools. Faith is powerful, but faith does not mean ignoring the root. Faith can also mean facing it with God beside you. I call those roots "Holes" we must identify what caused them, face it head on, forgive it and then leave it in the past.

I did not start seriously digging for the root cause of my pain until I was in my late thirties. I knew the two main incidents that traumatized me but I did not know how they were directly affecting my current life. I think my past left me with what I call "Holes" in my heart and soul and I did not know how to close them.

Unfortunately this world is filled with hurt people; people who have endured pain, death, loss, tragedy and disappointments of all kinds. I used to believe that I was alone in my despair and that my particular situation was rare. I thought no one else had experienced and could never understand it, so I never spoke about it. I was ashamed and I thought people would view me in a different light because of my past. Because I was unwanted and had been rejected by my mother, naturally I thought I would be rejected by the world in general. I always had my defenses up, which translated as attitude and reinforced the "angry black girl" trope for many. I was ok with that label, it kept me from bonding with people, it kept me safe. I had been hurt enough and was not about to allow anyone else to hurt me.

I had no idea how many hurt people there were in the world. Many people I have come in contact with have similar stories. I was ashamed of my past trauma and I thought people's knowledge of it would make them treat me differently. I also had no idea of how my issues with anger and depression were directly connected to my past. I simply thought I was crazy and was determined to keep my craziness a secret from the world.

When I was finally able to open up and begin to share my story with others, I realized that there were so many others in the world that have endured tragic circumstances. There were many abandoned children. There were many people living with un-diagnosed PTSD (Post-traumatic Stress Disorder). I realized that I was not alone, and that I wasn't crazy after all.

There are so many people in this world who have been hurt and abused and they are attempting to keep it together, never seeking the help needed to fully heal from their past, or even realizing that help exists. This is why sharing the tools that helped me with the readers of this book is so important to me.

I did not attempt to attack my issues until much later in life. I pray that by sharing my mental and emotional transformation tools with others, it won't take that long for another person to get the help they need, and they can begin living a happy, healthy life sooner than I did.

As I mentioned earlier, unfavorable life experiences have caused humans to develop what I describe as "Holes." I believe these holes are formed from past unresolved pain and trauma. I definitely walked around with gigantic holes in my heart for many years, and as time went on I began to realize many people were existing in life with these same holes, some even larger than mine.

If left untreated, these holes grow larger and deeper. Our lives continue to move forward and sometimes we go on living not realizing that these wounds are even there. We neglect to recognize that these scars have not only affected our lives, but the lives of everyone around us. They prevent us from giving and receiving love the way God intended for it to be. We were born to love naturally, wholeheartedly and without fear, but when we have been denied love from the beginning of our lives holes form in our hearts.

I personally believe that small pieces of our soul escape through those holes and we spend our entire lives trying to retrieve them and piece ourselves back together again. We try to mend our holes and our wounds with other people. Unfortunately during this process of trying to heal, we hurt other people, sometimes unintentionally. We can be completely oblivious to the pain we are causing others. There were times when I had no idea why I reacted so explosively to certain situations. My friends and family had no idea either. They just chalked it up to me being a crazy hot head.

One day my ex husband made a harmless, casual comment about liking the way a particular pair of shoes looked on a woman we saw in passing at the mall. I know he meant no harm whatsoever, but due to the holes in my heart, I interpreted his comment as if he was saying he wished I looked like her. In my mind, this meant he thought I wasn't good enough for him. We had such a secure relationship, he didn't think there would be any problem with commenting on another woman's shoes, and there shouldn't have been. Under normal circumstances there would not have been, but my holes were still untreated so you can imagine how I reacted; I exploded! Later that day, I went into the house and took every single pair of shoes I could find

41

and threw them at him screaming, *"Since you like her shoes so much and you don't like mine then here you go!"* He and I laugh about this today, but but it wasn't funny then.

Since my mother didn't love me, I was afraid that no one would. Although I had people in my life that clearly loved me, I had not yet learned to completely love myself, and would never be able to love him and accept love from him until I closed my holes.

Since I took the time to dissect my issues, I have grown so much. That growth started with identifying what my triggers were and why they existed. I had to dig deep into my past and connect the dots. Doing that work can be painful, but in the end, it will allow you to live a better quality of life.

Another example of how my "Holes" affected my personal relationships was when I was eighteen years old, less than a year after my grandmothers murder. My older sister had gone off to University of California, San Diego to attend college. I was living with my Aunt SaBra whom i was named after, my father's only sister and the only daughter to the grandmother that raised me. After my grandmother's funeral, I was still in the my aunt took on the responsibility of raising me. She owned a four-unit apartment building on 94th and Normandie. She moved me in with her. My father's older brother Charles Fisher also lived on the property.

We didn't have a lot of family left and I was still in a very fragile state. My sister Mary called home from college to say she would not be coming home for Thanksgiving and Christmas. Now this is actually a normal thing for a new college student. She was adjusting to her new life, and aside from being a student she had gotten a new job, but because of the untreated "holes" in my heart, I was devastated by the fact that my only sister was not coming home. I felt so alone, and although her decision had absolutely nothing to do with me, I wasn't emotionally strong enough to view it any other way than yet another abandonment.

All I knew was I needed her, I missed her, she was all I had. I cried so hard because she couldn't come, I ranted and raved. I wasn't emotionally secure enough to understand that she simply had work and school and it wasn't convenient for her to return to Los Angeles at that time. She was also still grieving from the loss of our beloved grandmother whom we had just buried in May.

I reacted the way I did solely because I had severe fears of loss. Our father was gone. Our mother was still addicted to drugs and absent from our lives. We lost the only consistent person in our lives that loved us. We were instantly snatched out of the home we grew up in and our lives were in disarray.

The cause of my erratic behavior was much deeper than I could understand, but it would be years before I would even scratch the surface of the psychological causes.

Once I did, I came to accept that because I had been abandoned, I did not feel valuable.

Nothing actually changes in our lives until we recognize and acknowledge our wounds and actually begin to deal with them. Physical scrapes and scratches will begin the natural healing process on their own; nature heals them in a few days with or without our help. Mental and emotional scars on the other hand, the ones we can't see require conscious action from us to get better.

Whatever method is needed for you to work on closing your holes, I urge you to identify and utilize it. Doing so will enhance the quality of your life. It will bring you a certain level of peace that many victims of abuse don't believe they will ever experience.

For me, forgiveness was a key part of filling in my holes. I needed to forgive my mother for abandoning me. Once I started to work on that, the gigantic gaping hole that I had gotten so used to camouflaging began to close.

The truth is, many people carry trauma and call it personality. You call it being independent, but really you learned not to trust anyone. You call it being guarded, but really you got hurt when you were open. You call it being strong, but really you were never allowed to be soft. You call it being private, but really you do not feel safe being seen. You call it being chill, but really you have learned to numb yourself so you do not fall apart. When you begin to tell the truth about what you carry, you begin to see yourself clearly. When you see yourself clearly, you can finally start giving yourself what you needed back then.

Some of you have been trying to heal without acknowledging what happened to you. You have been trying to move forward while pretending you were not affected. You have been trying to forgive while you are still bleeding. You have been trying to be okay for everyone else while your inner child is still waiting to be comforted. The truth is, you cannot heal what you will not name. Naming the pain is not making it bigger. Naming the pain is giving it a place to go. It is giving it language. It is giving it direction. It is bringing it out of your body and into the light where it can finally be processed instead of stored.

There is also a spiritual side to this. Because trauma can distort the way you see God. If you were hurt by someone who was supposed to protect you, you may struggle to trust God's protection. If you were abandoned, you may struggle to believe God stays. If you were judged harshly, you may struggle to believe God is gentle. If you were controlled, you may struggle to surrender. Trauma can twist your theology into fear. You may love God, but still expect punishment. You may pray, but still feel undeserving. You may believe in blessings, but still feel like you are the exception. That is why healing the root is not just emotional, it is spiritual. God is not asking you to carry distorted beliefs about Him. He wants to heal the way you see Him too.

Finding the root also means noticing your patterns without shaming yourself. Every pattern has an origin story. The way you cope did not come out of nowhere. The way you shut down was learned. The way you stay busy was learned. The way you avoid conflict was learned. The way you pick the wrong people over and over was learned. The way you over give and allow others to take advantage of you was learned. The way you keep quiet when you should speak up, was a learned behavior. Patterns are protection strategies that became habits. They were created when you needed them. But what protected you then may be poisoning you now, and you do not have to hate yourself for that. You just have to be honest enough to change.

It takes courage to go to the root because roots are under-ground. Roots are hidden. Roots are where you buried things you were not ready to feel. But let me tell you what happens when you heal the root. You stop reacting like you are still in the past. You stop living as if the worst thing is always about to happen again. You stop giving your power to old memories. You stop interpreting every moment through old pain. You start responding from the present. You start building your life from truth instead of fear.

Here is the part I need you to hear with your whole spirit. Finding the root is not meant to break you. It is meant to free you. It is meant to explain why you have been carrying what you have been carrying. It is meant to release shame. Because shame says, Something is wrong with me. But truth says, Something happened to me. Shame says, I am weak. But truth says, I adapted. Shame says, I am broken. But truth says, I am wounded and healing is possible. The truth changes the conversation you have with yourself, and the conversation you have with yourself changes your life.

You deserve to heal deeply, not just temporarily. You deserve to stop treating depression like a mystery and start understanding the story behind it. You deserve to stop blaming yourself for the way your body and mind respond when they have been through too much. You deserve to find the root and pull it up gently, with compassion, with support, with prayer, and with patience.

Because you are not just trying to feel better. You are trying to live better. You are trying to breathe again. You are trying to become whole. Please believe me when I tell you that it is possible. Peace of Mind, Happiness, Prosperity and the the most beautiful Self-Love is possible for us all.

5

Getting Out of Bed Again:

Depression has a way of turning your bed into both refuge and trap at the same time. Sliding under the covers can feel like protection from a world that suddenly seems overwhelming, yet staying there too long can make the walls close in. The noise of responsibility waits on the other side of the room, and your mind starts racing before your body even moves. A running list forms without permission-what needs to be done, what was left undone, what you should have handled better, what feels impossible to face. By the time morning officially begins, discouragement has already settled in. This has nothing to do with laziness or a lack of care. It comes from a place much deeper. Emotional exhaustion weighs on you in a way that sleep cannot fix, and that kind of fatigue can make you question whether you will ever feel normal again.

If this is familiar territory, understand something important: standing up anyway is not minor. It may look ordinary to someone else, but when depression is pressing down on you, that first step onto the floor carries real effort. Strength does not always roar; sometimes it shows up quietly in the decision to move when everything inside you wants to stay still. People who have never carried this kind of invisible weight might struggle to understand why basic tasks feel so heavy. That does not make your experience dramatic or exaggerated. Depression shifts the way your body feels, the way your thoughts circulate, and the way your heart responds to everyday life. Even so, you are still here. You are still searching. You are still open enough to read, to reflect, and to hope for something better. That matters more than you realize.

There is another lie depression likes to tell, and it usually comes in extremes. It suggests that if you cannot fix everything at once, then nothing is worth attempting. That mindset steals progress before it even begins. Real healing rarely arrives in grand gestures. It grows through steady, manageable steps that may seem insignificant to others but feel monumental to you. Choosing to shower. Answering one message. Stepping outside for five minutes of fresh air. Those moments count. Momentum is built from actions that look small on the surface but create movement beneath it. Celebrating those efforts is not settling; it is strengthening. Momentum begins quietly and builds over time. Keep honoring each step forward, because the larger victories you are hoping for are built on those early, faithful decisions.

Sometimes the first small win is opening your eyes and not immediately judging yourself for being alive. Sometimes the first win is sitting up. Opening the curtains and allowing the sun to come int. Sometimes it's swinging your legs over the side of the bed. Sometimes it's putting your feet on the floor and whispering, I'm going to try. Sometimes it's drinking water. Sometimes it's washing your face. Sometimes it's making your bed not because you feel amazing, but because you want to change the energy in the room. Sometimes it's stepping outside for two minutes and letting the air touch your skin. Sometimes it's answering one text. Sometimes it's eating something small. Sometimes it's taking your medicine or calling your therapist. Sometimes it's praying one honest sentence. Small wins are sacred because they are acts of self-respect when you feel like you have none.

You have to change the way you measure progress. Depression makes you compare yourself to who you were on your best day. It makes you compare yourself to people who aren't fighting the same battle. It makes you feel like you're failing because you can't keep up. But your progress is not measured by perfection. Your progress is measured by return. By the fact that you keep coming back. You keep trying again. You keep choosing life again. You keep choosing a next step again. That is strength. That is resilience. That is victory.

There is something spiritual about small wins because they require humility. They require you to accept that you are in a season where you must take your time. They urge you to stop rushing the process. They encourage you to stop shaming yourself for not being "back to normal" yet. Sometimes depression is the season where God teaches you how to be gentle with yourself. How to listen to your body and rest without guilt. How to stop performing. How to stop pretending you can carry everything and everybody. You matter most. Sometimes healing begins when you finally admit, I need help, and you stop arguing with your own needs. The burden of depression is too big to carry alone. Even if it's just one person. Reach out to them.

Eventually you will rebuild trust with yourself and the world around you. Depression breaks that trust. It makes you doubt your ability to follow through. It makes you feel unreliable to yourself. You make plans and then you cancel them. You promise yourself you'll do something and you don't. You start believing you can't even count on yourself. That belief can be crushing. Don't believe the lies. This too shall pass. Every small win is a deposit. Every time you do one tiny thing, you are telling yourself, I can trust me again. I am still here. I am still trying. I am still capable. You are rebuilding a relationship with yourself, and that relationship is part of your recovery. You have to become your biggest cheerleader.

If you are going to get out of bed again, you have to stop waiting for motivation to arrive like a visitor. Motivation often doesn't show up first. Movement shows up first. Action shows up first. The smallest action creates a spark, and the spark creates a little momentum. Depression makes you think you must feel better before you move, but sometimes you must move before you feel better. That movement can be tiny. It can be slow. It can be shaky. It can be imperfect. It still counts. Command yourself to get up and claim with your words that "Today is a Great day." Keep saying it and eventually it will be true.

Now let's talk about the shame that comes when you're in this kind of season. Shame will try to make you hide. Shame will try to make you isolate yourself from others. It will tell you that you should be embarrassed for struggling. It will tell you that other people can handle life, so why can't you. But shame is not your friend. It does not motivate you. On the contrary in will completely drain. Shame keeps you stuck in the bed because it makes you feel like you don't deserve to get up. The truth is, you deserve love and compassion. You deserve support. You deserve patience. You deserve to heal without being cruel to yourself. If no one is around to give you the love and compassion you need, you absolutely must give it to yourself.

Some days, getting out of bed again will require you to let go of the idea that you must do it alone. You may need a safe person who checks on you. You may need a counselor who helps you understand your patterns. You may need a doctor to help you regulate what depression has disrupted. You may need a routine that is designed for your nervous system, not for somebody else's. You may need to simplify your life until you can breathe. That is not failure. That is wisdom. That is the kind of strength that chooses survival and recovery over pride. It is wonderful if you do have these supportive people in your life. But I don't want you to be lost when they leave. you are the prize in your world. Forming dependencies on other human beings can create a deeper problem. In this book i want you to learn the importance of bringing yourself out of those dark places.

I also want to speak to the part of you that feels like your life has been on pause. Depression can make you feel like you are losing time. Like you are getting older and falling behind. Like everyone else is moving forward and you're stuck in a slow-motion version of yourself. But hear me clearly, Please!. Rest is not wasted time when your soul is rebuilding. Healing is not delay. Healing is preparation. Healing is restoration. Healing is you becoming strong in a new way. Not strong for the world, but strong for you. If there is a day when you just can not get up. Lay there and listen to a uplifting YouTube video. Try Les Brown, Zig Ziglar, Wayne Dyer, Sadhguru, Shi Heng Yi, Maya Angelou, Tim Robbins, Joyce Meyers, Eric Et Thomas.

Small wins save you because they prove that hope can exist in small doses. You don't need to feel a sudden wave of joy to be healing. You don't need to wake up one day completely free to be progressing. You need a little light. A small smile at yourself in the bathroom mirror. A deep long breath. A little movement at a time. A little love and support. Repeat those little things until they become a pattern and a path towards self-love.

One day, you will look back and realize your comeback was not one dramatic moment. It was a collection of small wins that nobody saw. The days you got up even though you didn't want to. The moments you chose to eat even though you had no appetite. The times you stepped outside even though you wanted to disappear. The prayers you whispered when you didn't have big faith. The boundaries you set when you were tired of being drained. The phone calls you finally made. The tears you finally let fall. The truth you finally told. Those were your turning points.

So if today all you can do is sit up, let that be enough. If today all you can do is breathe and say, I'm trying, let that be enough. If today all you can do is survive, let that be enough. You are not behind. You are healing. Healing is spiritual internal work.

6

Tools for the Hard Moments

Depression can feel like a out of control spiral. A spiral is one of the most exhausting parts of depression because it feels like you're being pulled downward by something you can't see. One thought turns into ten. One memory opens the door to a whole hallway of regret and sadness. A bad moment in the morning convinces you the whole day is ruined. Someone disappoints you and your mind starts whispering that nothing will ever change. Then before you realize what happened, you're not just sad, you're drowning in sorrow. You're not just tired, you feel hopeless. You're overwhelmed and you're questioning your whole life. You find yourself beating yourself up over every bad decision you have ever made. That is the spiral. It is fast. It is persuasive. It is emotionally unstable, and it tries to make you believe that every bad thought you have is the truth. Call it the devil, dark negative energy or whatever you choose. But recognizing when it has hold of you is a huge step in conquering it.

Here is what I need you to know, with love: a spiral is not some profound prophecy. A spiral is simply a pattern of negative thoughts and emotions. Patterns can be interrupted. There is no pattern you have formed that you cannot break. There is always a new start. No matter how deep you've gone down that rabbit hole, you can come back from it, as long as you have breath in your body.

Hard moments will come. That's not pessimistic, that's honest. Healing doesn't mean you'll never have another heavy day. Healing means you will learn what to do when the heavy day shows up. It means you stop letting one hard moment become a whole identity. It means you stop letting your mind run wild without being able to consciously reel it back in and take control of your thoughts. Healing means you learn how to take your power back in real time, even if your hands are shaking and your heart feels tired.

You can go from mental and emotional poverty to power. That power is inside of all of us. We all possess the ability to influence our thoughts and emotions. You simply, first, have to believe that you are in control, and secondly, you must learn the tools to activate the power inside of you.

And let me be clear: this is not about religion. So it does not matter if you call that power God, Universe, Yahweh, Ala, Ra, Chi, Divine Consciousness or Prana. Every human being, no matter what religion they are, has this amazing power within them. Every human being has unseen energy moving through them, and it is capable of working in their favor.

No one group of people is more deserving of blessings and love. We are all the same in worth, no matter what our belief system is. I use the word God in this book because that is my belief, but everyone is worthy and entitled to the same joy, the same good health, and the same prosperity, no matter what race, gender, economic status, or religion they are. I do not want you for one minute to think that if you have different beliefs, Or because you use a different word to describe the Divine Source that you are now stuck in the spiral of depression with no help. You are not. You are a powerful being with limitless potential. Do not allow society, or anyone, to make you believe you deserve less because you believe differently. We can all have a great life. We can all rise and be happy and successful. We can all live up to our fullest potential. The most significant belief you need to ensure a great quality of life is your belief in yourself. Believe that you are worthy of everything this amazing world has to offer, No Matter What!

One of the first reasons spirals get so strong is because you treat the thoughts you have during them like the are facts. Depression doesn't just drop a thought, it drops a conclusion. It says, "You're not enough," and you accept it. It says, "Nobody cares," and you accept it. It says, "You'll always be like this," and you accept it. The moment you accept it, your body responds like it's true. Your shoulders tighten. Your chest gets heavy. Your appetite shifts. Your energy crashes. Your entire energetic vibration lowers and your uncontrolled emotions flood in. That is why the spiral feels physical, because your body is reacting to a story.

This chapter is about changing the story before it takes over the room, before it takes over your life. Sometimes stopping the spiral begins with something that sounds almost too simple. You simply pause and take a deep breath. You identify what's happening int that moment. You stop calling it your personality and you start calling it what it is. You say, "This is a spiral." You say, "This is depression talking." You say, "My nervous system is activated." You say, "I am triggered right now." Naming it is not weakness. Naming it is acknowledging it. You cannot fight what you won't identify. You cannot heal what you wont admit is happening. That one of the first steps.

I used to describe depression as a tennis ball traveling quickly at my head. As I began to heal, I realized that I was holding the tennis racket. I imagined taking a firm stance, racket in hand and swatting that tennis ball far away with everything in me. This worked for me. Create a visual for yourself of winning the war with depression and use that visual when you feel it coming on.

When you are in a hard moment, your mind wants to time travel. It wants to drag you into the past and punish you with memories. Or it wants to drag you into the future and terrify you with "what if." The spiral feeds on time travel. It gets stronger when you leave the present. So one of the most powerful things you can do is come back to right now. Not tomorrow. Not last year. Not five minutes from now, right now. Bring yourself right back into the present moment. Begin to tell yourself that you are safe in this moment. You are breathing in this moment. You are still here in this moment. That is enough, be patient with yourself.

This is where spirituality becomes more than a concept. This is where God becomes more than a belief. Because in the hard moments, you need something steady, something higher than your feelings and stronger than the lie. Depression will try to make you believe you are alone, but you are not alone. Even if you feel lonely, you are not abandoned. Even if you feel far from God, He is not far from you. Feelings shift, but God remains the same always. The spiral is loud, but it has no authority over a strong, confident mind anchored in truth.

And here is what makes that truth so powerful: faith is not pretending you don't hurt, it's refusing to let hurt become your identity. It's being able to say, "This is heavy," without also saying, "This is hopeless." It's learning how to sit in the storm without surrendering to it. Your emotions may feel real in the moment, but they are not the final verdict on your life. Just like all things, there is a season, and it will pass. The darkness may visit, but it does not get to move in. The feelings may rise, but they do not get to rule. When you hold onto God in the hard moments, through prayer, through breath, through one honest sentence at a time, you are building spiritual stability, and stability is what carries you until the light shows up again.

Hard moments can make you speak against yourself. That's another way the spiral wins. You start labeling yourself. You start saying, "I'm stupid." "I'm broken." "I'm a mess." "I can't do anything right." And every word you speak becomes a weight you carry. So in the hard moments, your mouth matters. Not because you're pretending, but because you're fighting for your life. Your mouth can either feed the spiral or starve it. Your mouth can either keep you trapped or help you climb. You don't need fancy words. You need strong words. You need words that hold you up. Words like, "I am having a hard moment, but I will make it through." or "Today is difficult but tomorrow will be better." Words like, "This is heavy, but it is temporary." Words like, "I have survived worse than this." Words like, "I am not quitting on myself today." or "I'm getting better and better everyday."

Sometimes stopping the spiral means choosing one simple

action that returns you to your body. Depression can pull you into your head so deeply that you forget you have a body that can help you regulate. Your body can become your anchor. Your breath can become your rope. Your senses can become your ladder. When the spiral is trying to pull you under, coming back into your body can save you. Even small things can become healing tools. Water on your face. Sunlight on your skin. Sitting upright. Opening a window. Stepping outside. Planting your bare feet in the grass. Putting your hand on your chest and reminding yourself, "I am here." These are not random tricks. These are ways of signaling safety to your system. The spiral cannot thrive as easily when your body is grounded.

Hard moments also expose what you need. Sometimes the spiral is a sign that you're depleted. Just like the body shows clear danger signs when you are depleted of water. The mind is the same way.

Sometimes the onset of depression is not even about a specific situation. Sometimes you're exhausted. Sometimes you haven't had real rest in weeks. Sometimes you've been giving too much and receiving too little. Sometimes you've been trying to be strong while ignoring your own needs. Depression loves depletion because depletion weakens your resistance. That's why taking care of your basic needs is not "selfish," it's warfare. It's protection. It's how you stay in the fight.

You also have to be careful about isolation during hard moments. Depression will tell you to disappear, to stop answering, to cancel everything, to retreat into silence. Sometimes you do need quiet. Sometimes you do need rest. But there is a difference between resting and hiding. The spiral gets stronger when you are alone with your darkest thoughts for too long. If you have one safe person, one prayer partner, one therapist, one friend

58

who understands, hard moments are the time to reach out. Not when you feel strong enough, but when you feel tempted to spiral deeper. You do not have to carry the hard moments by yourself.

I want you to understand something important. Stopping the spiral does not always look like suddenly feeling better. Be patient with yourself. Sometimes stopping the spiral looks like choosing not to go further down. It looks like preventing a bad hour from becoming a bad day. It looks like getting through the moment without harming yourself, without numbing yourself, without abandoning yourself. It looks like saying, "I'm not okay, but I'm still here." That is victory. That is progress. That is a tool working.

Now you are learning how to lead yourself through darkness. You are developing the skills to comfort yourself when you are down. You are learning how to pause instead of panic. In this book you learn how to interrupt the lie before it becomes your whole mood. It will teach you to recognize the warning signs and respond with care instead of shame. That is what mature healing looks like. It's not dramatic. It's consistent. It's brave. It's daily. But it is possible.

Let me say this with love. If your hard moments ever include thoughts of harming yourself, you deserve immediate support. You deserve someone to talk to right away. Not because you're weak, but because your life is precious. If you ever feel like you are in danger, call your local emergency number or reach out to a crisis hotline in your area. In the United States, you can call or text 988 for the Suicide and Crisis Lifeline. You don't have to explain everything perfectly. You just have to reach. Help is not something you earn. Help is something you deserve.

You are not meant to fight alone or spiral in silence. You do not have to carry the weight without support. You are meant to heal and live a happy, prosperous life. You are meant to rise up like a phoenix from everything that you have been through and feel light, happy and free again. The hard moments are real, but they are not the end of your story. They are simply moment that you are now learning how to move through without letting them steal your future.

One significant tool that worked for me when I was depressed was a book by Michael Singer called the "Untethered Soul." it was my first introduction to the fact that we have a little voice in our head, a internal voice that is not always guiding us correctly.

The internal voice is a product of your subconscious mind. It is fueled by your fears and doubts until you learn to reprogram it. In this book I offer techniques that will assist you in reprogramming and officially declaring war on that negative voice in your head.

Declaring war and effectively winning that war with the enemy of the mind should be the ultimate goal. If the war is won with-in, all external enemies won't even have the ability to affect us. The true battle is in the mind. Gaining the abilities to control our thinking patterns. Learning to master control of our thoughts will allow us the privilege of only accepting thoughts that serve us well to enter into our mind space and we will develop the ability to cast out negative thoughts and images because they are the true internal enemy.

Maintaining a persistent negative thinking pattern will prove to be more harmful to you than anything you can ever encounter in your life. We must learn the tools needed to declare all out war on anything that prevents us from leading a happy fulfilling life. This is one of the main reasons why I felt compelled to write this book. It is my desire to share with the world the tools that helped me change my negative mindset. Developing these tools are the reason I will never be depressed again. This is my prayer for you as well.

The first step in changing self-deprecating internal dialogue is identifying it. What has the enemy of the mind been repeatedly saying to you? What has the internal enemy convinced you of that simply is not true?.

7

Your Body Is Talking: Sleep, Food, Movement, and Mood

Depression is not only a battle in your mind. It lives in your body too. It changes your energy. It changes your appetite and your sleep. It zaps you of all motivation. It causes you to feel heavy and unattractive. It takes over as soon as you wake up. When you are depressed you become easily irritated. The smallest things frustrate you and cause you to shut down. It makes you want to isolate yourself from the rest of the world.

It makes you feel like a worthless failure. But you are not. Do not believe any of that, although I know from experience that it does feel real. I wish I could prove to you that you will feel better with each passing day and eventually depression will never knock on your door again.

Your body is always communicating. It talks through fatigue and tension. It talks to you through headaches and stomach issues. It talks through restlessness. It talks through craving a unnecessary amount of food. It talks through numbness. It talks through that feeling of being "off" even when you cannot explain it. Depression can make you feel like your emotions have no logic or reason, but often your body is carrying the reason. Sometimes your mind is not being dramatic. Sometimes your body is dysregulated. The most powerful thing you can do is stop judging yourself and start listening.

Sleep is one of the first places depression shows up. Either you cannot sleep, or you sleep too much, and even after a full night you still feel tired. Depression can make your mind race at night and crash during the day. It can make your body feel heavy like it is filled with sand. It can make you dread the night because the quiet time gives your thoughts room to get loud. When your sleep gets disrupted, your mood gets more fragile. Everything feels harder when you are tired. Your patience gets shorter. Your confidence gets lower. Your emotions become quicker to flood. It becomes easier to spiral. That is not weakness. That is biology. Your brain cannot regulate well without rest.

But here is the part that gives you power. You do not have to fix your entire sleep life overnight to start healing. You just need to treat sleep like it matters. Because it does. Try to develop a feeling of gratitude for sleep. Depression will tell you to stay up scrolling, to stay in your head, to stay wired, to stay distracted, to avoid quiet. But your healing requires rest. Not just physical rest, but nervous system rest. Sometimes the most spiritual thing you can do is create a softer night. A calmer, peaceful routine. A bedtime that honors your mind and body instead of punishing them. Rest is not laziness. Rest is repair. Your body is replenishing itself. Find positive affirmations on YouTube and listen to them while you are attempting to fall asleep. This was a tool that worked wonders for me.

A lot of people over eat when they are down and others lose their appetite completely. The ones who eat constantly, it is not because they are hungry, but because they are trying to soothe something. Depression can make you crave sugar, carbs, and comfort foods, because your body is searching for quick relief. Then shame shows up. You judge yourself for eating too much or eating too little. But shame does not heal the body. Shame weakens it. Your body needs nourishment to fight. Your brain needs fuel to regulate. When you are depressed, eating can feel like work, but every time you nourish yourself, you are telling your system, I care about you. You are telling your body, We are not giving up.

Movement is one of the most misunderstood parts of depression recovery. People hear "exercise helps" and it can feel insulting when you can barely get out of bed. But movement does not have to mean a gym, a workout plan, or a perfect routine. Movement is simply telling your body, we are still alive. It can be stretching in your bed. It can be walking to the mailbox. It can be standing in the sunlight for a few minutes. It can be dancing in your kitchen for one song. Sometimes its slow small movements. But movement changes chemistry. Movement moves stuck energy. It helps your nervous system discharge what it has been holding. Depression often makes your body freeze, and gentle movement helps you thaw out.

Mood is not only emotional. Mood is physical too. Your hormones and stress levels matter. Your blood sugar matters. How much water you drink makes a difference because hydration is vital. Your vitamins matter. Adequate sunlight makes a huge difference in your mood. Your nervous system matters. That is why you can wake up and feel heavy for no obvious reason. That is why your mood can drop after days of poor sleep. That is why you can feel anxious when you have not eaten. You feel irritable when you are dehydrated. Sometimes the enemy is not your character and your mood may not be the result of a situation.

Sometimes the enemy is your body needing care.

This chapter is not here to make you feel like you need to become perfect to heal. It is here to remind you that healing is possible. Each day you get up is progress. You are not a floating spirit separated from your body. You are one system. Your system deserves patience and compassion. When you begin caring for your body, you are not being shallow. You are being wise by giving yourself a stronger foundation to do the emotional work. You are making the battle easier by strengthening the vessel you live in.

Spiritually, this matters because your body is not an afterthought. Your body is sacred. Your body has carried you through things you do not even talk about. It has survived heartbreak. It has survived trauma. Your body has survived disappointment, grief, and stress. It has still shown up for you even when you did not know how to show up for yourself. So when depression tries to make you hate your body, neglect your body, punish your body, ignore your body, you have to remember that your body is not your enemy. Your body is your partner in healing. It is the beautiful vessel that houses your infinite spirit.

Sometimes the most powerful prayer is not just asking God to remove depression. Sometimes the prayer is asking God to teach you how to care for yourself. How to slow down and gain control of your thoughts. How to rest without guilt. How to eat with love. How to move with gentleness. How to listen. How to notice what your body is saying before it has to scream. Because your body will eventually scream if it is ignored long enough. Many people call it depression when it is actually years of unprocessed stress living in the body.

You are allowed to rebuild your life through care and self-love.

You are allowed to create a routine that supports your healing. You can take your mental health seriously and you are allowed to see your sleep as a priority. You are allowed to feed yourself without shame. You are allowed to move without pressure. You are allowed to treat your body like it deserves to be here. Because it does.

I need you to understand this. Caring for your body is not separate from your healing journey. It is part of the journey. The more you honor your body, the more your mood has a chance to stabilize. The more stable your mood becomes, the more clearly you can think, and controlling how you think is detrimental to your healing. When your thoughts are clear the easier it becomes to break the thought cycle. The easier it becomes to stop the spiral. The easier it becomes to face triggers with wisdom. Your body and your mind are connected, and when you support one, you support the other.

So if all you can do today is drink water and breathe, let that be a win. If all you can do is eat something small, let that be a win. If you are able to take a short walk to the end of the driveway, that's definitely a win. Your healing is not measured by huge leaps. It is measured by consistent care. It is measured by showing up for yourself in small ways until the small ways become your new normal.

8

Boundaries Are Healing: Protecting Your Peace

Depression is not always caused by what is inside you. Sometimes it is what or who keeps reaching you. Sometimes it is what or who keeps draining you. Quite often it is what keeps demanding more than you can give, and what keeps getting access to your head and your heart without permission. When you have been living without boundaries, your spirit becomes tired in a way that sleep cannot fix, because sleep restores the body, but boundaries, if we set them, restore the soul. If you are serious about healing, you have to be serious about protecting your own peace. I have had to set hard boundaries with many of my friends and family. I won't say the decision to do so is an easy one. However, it is vital when you are trying to save your own life.

A boundary is not about shutting people out. It is about deciding what you will allow into your space and what you will not. Without boundaries, kindness turns into being taken advantage of and support turns into exhaustion. Generosity loses its meaning when it constantly leaves you drained. Many people avoid setting boundaries because they believe it makes them harsh or selfish. They worry that saying no will disappoint others or damage relationships. In reality, boundaries are not about punishment or rejection. They are about clarity. They communicate what you value, what you can handle, and where your limits are. Healthy boundaries protect your energy so that when you do show up for others, you are doing it from strength instead of resentment.

When I was still quite emotionally broken, I allow friends and family to use me. I paid for all the dinners and offered financial support to able-bodied adults who took me for granted. Because I was so desperate for love, I did it willingly. Once I healed that all stopped lol. Once you learn to love yourself, you notice that some people would not to the same for you if you needed them.

Depression often grows in people who are always giving and rarely receiving, people who are always showing up for others and rarely being poured into, people who are always listening and rarely being heard, people who carry everybody's emotions while their own emotions stay locked up. When you live like that, you can become emotionally bankrupt. Then you start blaming yourself for not having energy, not having joy. You have no patience and no motivation. But you cannot keep pouring from an empty cup. At some point, your mind and body will force you to stop. Sometimes depression is that force. It is your system saying, I cannot keep doing this.

Protecting your peace begins with telling the truth about what drains you, not what drains other people, not what "shouldn't" bother you, but what actually drains you. Certain conversations drain you. There are many people in your life that drain you. You can be drained by certain environments. Having expectations of others will drain you. You have been trying to incessantly pray for those draining people when you actually need to protect yourself from them. Prayer is indeed powerful, but prayer does not replace wisdom. Pray for them from a distance. Prayer does not replace boundaries and it does not replace the decision to stop letting chaos have constant access to you.

Some of you were taught that love means unlimited access. I definitely felt that way. We are raised to believe that family means you endure anything. That being a good friend means you always say yes. That being a good partner means you tolerate disrespect. That being spiritual means you never get upset. That being positive means you never set limits. These are the biggest lies we ever told ourselves. it a person offers nothing but drama and turmoil to your life, you must back away from them. Love without boundaries becomes resentment, and resentment is heavy. It sits in your chest. You find yourself-talking to yourself throughout the day, saying all the things you wish you would have said. Sticking up for yourself in your head because you did not have the courage to actually do it. That makes you tired and irritable. It makes you shut down. It makes you feel guilty for feeling what you feel. Eventually, it can deepen depression because you start feeling trapped in a life that does not honor you.

I have a sister whose adult behavior is disrespectful and toxic. I wanted to build a closer relationship with her because we were not raised together. However, every time she came around, she acted as if I owed her something, almost like she felt entitled and had the idea that I was financially responsible for her, and she was in her forties. I tolerated it for a while because she was my blood, but eventually I had to distance myself from her. I'm still open to a relationship, but I have done so much work to heal from all of my past trauma that I have little to no patience for her antics. I pray that changes one day, because I truly would love for us to enjoy a peaceful, sisterly relationship.

Boundaries are healing because they teach your nervous system safety. When you have no boundaries, your body stays on edge. You never know when someone will call with drama, like the sister I described earlier. You never know when someone will need something. You never know when someone will demand your attention. You never know when someone will cross the line again. That unpredictability creates stress. Stress creates exhaustion. Exhaustion creates vulnerability. Depression loves vulnerability. When you set boundaries, your body relaxes and your mind quiets. Your spirit breathes easier and deeper, not because life becomes perfect, but because your life becomes protected.

There is also a spiritual reason boundaries matter. You cannot grow in environments that keep cutting you down. You cannot heal around people who keep reopening your wounds. You cannot hear God clearly when you are surrounded by noise, manipulation, and pressure. Boundaries are not just emotional decisions. They are spiritual alignment. Some people simply are not meant to be in your life. They are not part of your path. You must choose peace over performance. They are you choosing health over guilt. They are you choosing wisdom over fear. They are you trusting that God will still love you even when you say no.

One of the hardest parts about boundaries is accepting that some people will not like them. Many will say that you think you are better than them. People who benefited from your lack of boundaries will resist when you finally create them. People who are used to you over-giving will act like you changed. People who are used to you being available for them, will guilt you when you take a step back. The ones who are used to you saying yes will get uncomfortable when you say no. Depression will try to convince you that their discomfort means you are wrong. But their discomfort may simply mean they can no longer control you. Healing often requires disappointment, not your disappointment, but theirs. You will disappoint people when you stop abandoning yourself and put yourself first. That is a part of recovery. Do not be afraid to pour all the energy you have into yourself. It is what you need to have the strength to master *"Kicking Depression in the Butt"*

I have four amazing children, one son and three daughters, and I absolutely adore them. One key component I learned in maintaining positivity is putting myself first. Yes, I know most parents spend their entire lives putting their kids first. That is what we are taught to do. However, if you do not put yourself first, you are in no mental and emotional condition to give your children the best version of you.

When I was a younger parent, I thought my feelings and needs did not matter as long as the kids were happy. Most parents think this way. They believe they must sacrifice everything because they chose to be parents. That was definitely how I felt. Now I feel differently. There is so much work that needs to be done to live a happy, peaceful life. If you neglect yourself and only focus on making your children happy, you will look up and find yourself a senior citizen who is sad, depressed, and unfulfilled. Your children will have married and gone on with their own lives, checking in with you only on holidays, busy creating their world. Making sure your own emotional and mental needs are covered first is not selfish. Life goes on after parenthood. I now know how important it is to make sure I am happy as well.

71

Because of my past, I have grown up with many emotional deficiencies. I felt unwanted, and my self-esteem was very low. I became a parent long before I even attempted to seek healing from my past. Because I still carried so much past trauma, my love for my kids was what I considered unhealthy. I was a great parent by society's standards. I worked hard and provided everything they wanted and needed. I even tried to make sure I showed plenty of affection and attended to the best I knew how to all of their emotional needs. I encouraged and uplifted them, hugged and kissed them regularly, and I went to all their school functions and always showed up for them as a mother. As far as I was concerned, I was the best parent ever.

However, that didn't leave any time for me to attend to my own needs. Honestly, I can't say that in my early twenties and thirties, I even realized I had unattended emotional and mental needs. Although I knew I had been through trauma, I didn't know I could seek help from the recurring memories and pain. I didn't know many of my fears and reactions to certain situations were direct results of the trauma I had experienced. I didn't realize the obsessive way in which I loved my children was rooted in fear and trauma.

Protecting your peace also means recognizing that you are allowed to outgrow relationships. You are allowed to outgrow conversations. You can outgrow environments that keep you in survival mode. You can evolve from the version of you who tolerated everything. Stop negotiating with disrespect. Stop letting others hurt and abuse your kindness. No longer serve as someone's emotional punching bag. You are allowed to stop being the fixer of everyone else and solely concern yourself with fixing you. You are allowed to stop being the one who holds everyone together while you secretly fall apart inside. This is not about becoming cold. This is about becoming whole.

Sometimes the boundary is **external.** You stop answering late-night calls. You limit contact. You stop explaining yourself to people who twist your words. You stop going places that trigger you. You stop allowing certain conversations to continue. You stop giving your time to people who only call when they need something. You stop letting your phone become an emergency room for everybody else's emotions. These boundaries create space in your life, and space is where healing grows.

Sometimes the boundary is **internal.** You stop letting guilt make your decisions. You stop replaying what they said. You stop trying to prove your worth to yourself and others. You stop taking responsibility for other people's feelings. You stop blaming yourself for someone else's behavior. You stop negotiating your needs down to nothing. You stop abandoning yourself in order to be loved by others. Internal boundaries are powerful because they protect your peace even when life is loud.

When you start protecting your peace, you will notice something. Your energy returns in small waves. Your mind begins to clear. Your emotions become less intense. You start feeling more like you. You may even start hearing your own voice again, the voice you buried under everybody else's needs and expectations, the voice that knows what you need, the voice that knows what you can handle, the voice that knows when something is too much. Depression often mutes that voice. Boundaries bring it back.

When the healing process begins, you no longer view everything as an attack against you. Your perspective widens to accommodate the feelings and points of view of others. It is currently December 23, 2025 and I continued working on myself. I continued putting myself first. That is what I want for each of

73

you.

Today, I have healed many of my wounds. I used to call them "holes," which we all have, some are larger than others. Today, at age fifty-six, many of the gigantic "holes" left from the hurt and abuse that I walked around with are closed. I know not that I'm worthy of love and happiness, no matter how my life began. But that healing didn't drop out of the sky. I had to seek it out. I had to desire to stop viewing the world as horrid and me as its victim. I had to choose to stop being angry that I didn't have a perfect childhood. I had to forgive my parents for succumbing to their substance addictions.

Most importantly, I had to gain control over my thoughts. I had to practice replacing negative thoughts with positive ones, repeatedly, until it became a habit. That is the dream I have for you all. I dream you get to the point where I am now. Where you boldly and confidently say : *"I will Never be depressed again."* Do not give up because it is possible for you too.

Switching out the negative with the positive must become second nature to you. Your mind is the magical tool needed to transform your earthly experience into a happy, fulfilling one. We all deserve and can achieve happiness. Become better for yourself and no one else. Live for you; let every day's mission be for you to feel happiness and peace in every moment. You are the captain of your soul and your fate lies in your own hands. When you don't feel great, learn the tools to analyze and process the emotions you are having, then release them and move forward.

As long as you are alive, there will always be something that has the potential to cause you pain. Small, daily negative situations at home and work can, if you allow them to, can chip away at your happiness and peace. Acknowledge your feelings in every moment, learn from them, and proceed through life with your new found tools. Customize your tools for your life. Create personal affirmations specifically for your needs and the areas you want to improve in.

Throughout your daily life, you will have to pull many of those tools out of the toolbox to navigate through life and stay positive. Some of the transformational work may seem repetitive and tedious, but don't give up. Repetition is necessary to reprogram the mind. Commit the positive tools to habit, and soon you will rejoice in the evidence that they work. I assure you, you will see positive changes in your life and mindset.

When you struggle your entire life with love, or the absence of love, you form many unhealthy attachments. These attachments can cause you great pain. Because of being abandoned by my biological mother, my need for love was greater than others. Even though my mother's choices were drug-induced and perhaps "she wasn't in her right mind," it didn't prevent me from growing up feeling unwanted and unloved. Love is our true nature, and we shouldn't have to fight for it. We shouldn't have to live in constant fear of not being loved, and even when someone loves us, we shouldn't be afraid of losing their love.

This type of love is unhealthy. However, many people experience love in this unhealthy way. Until we do the emotional repairs on ourselves that are needed to learn to love without fear and teach ourselves how to have positive, healthy relationships, unfortunately, these are the relationships we will build with others. It may very well feel like love, but it is not. Love is kind. Love doesn't hurt. Until we let go of the belief that we don't deserve to be loved, our relationships with our parents, siblings, children, and spouses will all suffer. Every human being deserves to be loved. It took many years for me to realize that the possessive way I loved my children was coming from a place of fear. We have a fear of losing them because our love for them is so strong that we cannot bear the thought of being without them. However, we are loving them while carrying the wounds from our past that have yet to be healed.

Once I began healing and truly began knowing that I was a valuable person, my love lost the desperate undertone. By the time my children were adults, I was so full of self-love and admiration that small things like regular phone calls and holiday visits were no longer vital necessities. I was no longer crippled if they didn't reach out and assure me of their love. I finally loved myself. Loving myself became my primary focus. I enjoyed being in my own company. If my kids were busy with their own lives and didn't check in as much as I would have liked, I wouldn't take it personally, and it didn't crush my soul like it once would have. I could detach from that unhealthy, needy, can't live without them type of behavior. It does not mean your love for them has diminished. It simply means your love for yourself takes precedence over everything. You realize you too are the prize. You are a worthy, valuable being that adds to the lives of others as much as they do to yours. Arriving at this point in my life felt wonderful. People who have taught us to put everyone else and their needs before our own have done us a disservice. We can't truly love others until we master loving ourselves.

Breaking attachments productively is done in peace and love. It doesn't mean you love people any less. It isn't a negative "I'm done with them" situation. It means you no longer need their attention and presence the way you need food, water, and air. Other people do not control your life and emotional stability. It means that when you and a loved one don't agree on something, you no longer worry about the relationship being damaged and never seeing them again. I used to be afraid to voice an opposing opinion to my family. When you have those fear-based attachments, you find yourself not truly being yourself for fear of losing them. You become very passive and in agreement with things you very well might not agree with. You are subconsciously afraid to stand up for yourself or oppose anything because you think they will not love you anymore if you do. Although I lived that way for years, this is not a healthy way to love. I do not agree with explosive behavior of any kind, but there is always a kind, loving way to express your opinion or viewpoint on things. Your voice matters.

It took years for me to realize I was creating unhealthy attachments to friends, family, and lovers. They all feel like actual loving relationships until you truly know the difference. This is your world. If life is a play, you have the starring role. You should give no one the power to destroy your image of yourself. Let's say you run into a person you don't even know who is downright cruel, and this person says something mean to you like, "You're fat," or, "You are ugly." It is challenging to comprehend how a person can be so cruel when we are embodiment's of pure love. In the world we inhabit, there are many people who are truly hurting within themselves. Unfortunately, they will lash out at others. You could end up being the person they spew their evil onto that particular day. You must detach from their experience. It has nothing to do with you. You can't take anything they say about you to heart— their opinion of you is not a fact. How you feel about yourself is what matters. If we are honest with ourselves, we have all said something unkind to another person. I don't point that out to judge you, but to show you that we can choose to be better. We can identify the behavior in ourselves and others. We cannot change others, but we can change ourselves. We've all felt and inflicted the pain of hurtful words. Only then can we learn the lessons needed to understand it's all a choice—a choice to be mean to another, a choice to speak harsh words out of your mouth. We choose how we allow others to treat us. It is also a choice to avoid letting someone else's mistreatment affect our spirit, no matter who—parents, siblings, employers, spouses. Do not allow anyone to mistreat you. Usually, when we allow this behavior, it is because we have not recognized our worth. Regardless of who you are, you are worthy and deserving of love, respect, and kindness.

Detaching and setting boundaries comes in many forms. After twenty-six years, I changed the name of the salon I owned for twenty-six years. My Braiding salon took great care of me for years, but it was time for me to detach from the name "Braids By SaBrina" a name I advertised and worked hard to make a household name in the Los Angeles community. My staff and I drove the streets of Los Angeles in my burgundy H2 Hummer, flooding businesses, shopping centers, and parking lots with "Braids By SaBrina" flyers for many years. The decision to change the name and no longer offer the service of braiding wasn't an easy one. However, at this time in my life, I was dealing with a medical scare. After a tonsillectomy surgery the Doctor found a tumor called a Glomus Tympanicum. I knew in order for me to maintain a positive mindset while this tumor was still living in my head, I had to remove all negativity from my life. Four months earlier I had been feeling the urge for change anyway. I had given twenty-six years to the community, offering excellent service and giving jobs to over 1700 women, and even a few men in the Los Angeles community. I trained them all to be professional braiders and taught them how to advertise and sustain a business of their own.

There were many difficulties in being a consistent salon owner and governing over so many young people. It taught me to be a leader and showed me I could accomplish anything I set my mind to. I will be honest: I ruled with a stern "SaBrina's way or no way" motto. At five feet, two inches tall, I needed to establish authority or be run over by my many employees. I gave my all to that business, and I have no regrets. I will always be known as the famous "Braid Queen." To create a life of good health and peace, I had to eliminate the stress caused by my employees, getting them to take pride in the business and dealing with challenging attitudes and disrespectful behavior. As the salon owner, I was held accountable for their tardiness and rude attitudes. I had to address any of their mistakes with the clients because, after all, the salon was named Braids By SaBrina. I was young and a full-time mother, raising kids and trying to develop the young women who worked for me into potential business owners. It wasn't easy.

Finding out about the tumor had the potential to send me backwards emotionally. I vowed to never be depressed again so I knew I had to rid myself of the few very stressful employees I had left and create a environment of healing and peace until my surgery to remove the tumor. I sat down and prayed about it and God basically said "It's time, It's a New Day!. So seven days later I politely let go of the last for braiders, I changed all of the salons signs and fliers to "A New Vision Dreadlock Studio" and I never looked back. I worked in my salon alone for three more years. I serviced one client at a time. I was able to create a space of peace which prevented me from panicking every time I felt the tumor beating in my head. Yes it somehow was connected to my hearts rhythm. On January 2,3 and 4 of 2025. Dr. Ikera

Isiyama successfully removed the tumor with no complications.

Let me remind you of something that matters. You are not called to carry what is killing you. You do not have to stay connected to what is breaking you down. You must stop saying yes while your mental health suffers. Your peace is not optional. It is not a luxury. Your peace is a requirement for your healing. Protecting your peace is not selfish. It is responsible. You can love people and still need distance. You can forgive people and still set limits. You can be kind and still say no. You can be spiritual and still protect yourself. You can be a good person and still choose yourself. Boundaries are healing because they teach you that your life matters too. In fact, it matter most.take care of yourself first and learn to monitor your thoughts and control your emotions. Your future is at stake. When you finally start living like you matter, depression begins to lose its grip because you are no longer living in constant depletion.

9

Rewriting the Story: Identity Beyond Depression

Depression doesn't just affect how you feel. It tries to rename you. It tries to take one season of struggle and turn it into a permanent label. It tries to make you introduce yourself to life as broken, damaged, unworthy, complicated, too much for people to handle and not worthy enough for life. It takes your worst moments and claims them as your whole identity. It takes your hardest days and tries to convince you that this is the "real you." But depression is not allowed to define you. It may be something you are experiencing, but it is not who you are.

There is a difference between pain and identity. Pain is something you carry for a while. Identity is what you believe you are. Depression blurs that line. It makes you believe that because you feel heavy, you are heavy. Because you feel stuck, you are stuck. Because you feel hopeless, you are hopeless. But feelings are not facts. Feelings are signals and information. Feelings are waves. Waves are real, but they are not permanent. They go up and always come back down. Your identity is deeper than any wave. Your identity is what remains when the wave passes.

Rewriting the story begins when you stop letting depression narrate your life. Depression will tell the story like this. You've always been like this. You'll never change. You'll never heal. Nothing works. Nobody understands. You're all alone. It's too late for you. You missed your chance. It tells the story with a voice that sounds certain, because certainty is how it wins. It is a trick of the enemy and you are allowed to challenge that story. You are allowed to question it. You are allowed to interrupt it and say, Naw, that is not the whole truth. That is not the full story. This is temporary. That is not the final chapter of my life.

Your life is not one chapter. It is a book, and you are not finished writing yet. Sometimes depression grows stronger because you keep retelling the story of your life through the lens of what hurt you. You replay everything you lost. You replay everything that failed, who left you and who did you wrong. You replay all the disappointments and all the betrayals in your life. You remain focused on the years you feel you wasted. But if you are not careful, your mind starts writing a conclusion based on that painful story you keep telling. You can stop it in its tracks and write a new conclusion, not a fake one, not a rushed one, not one that you truly don't believe is possible or denies what happened. A true one that includes your resilience. A true one that includes your survival. Write one that includes God's protection, even when you didn't realize you were being protected. Write a story that includes the fact that you are still here. As I always say, as long as you have breath in your body, there is an opportunity for a new vision, a new you, a new identity.

There is something spiritual about identity because your identity is who you believe you are. Your state ID may say one thing, but who you truly are depends on what you tell yourself about you, how you speak over yourself and your life, and what you believe your future holds. For example, some people cannot even conceive of the possibility of prosperity; therefore, they live in poverty all of their lives. Depression wants you to agree with the lowest version of yourself. It wants you to claim defeat. It wants you to speak death and doom over your future. It wants you to accept a name that God never gave you, like dumb, broke, mean, ugly, lazy. But you were created with purpose and in the image of God. You were created with value and love. You were created with a purpose, and even if you cannot see it clearly right now, you are still who God said you are. Depression can cover the light, but it cannot remove it for good.

This is where you begin to separate yourself from the struggle. You stop saying, I am depressed, like it is a permanent label and you start saying, I am experiencing depression, and I am healing, my condition is temporary. You stop saying, I am broken and you start saying, I have been wounded, and I am recovering. You stop saying, I am a mess and you start saying, I am getting stronger daily. You stop speaking like you are your diagnosis. You stop speaking like you are your worst day. Start speaking like you are a human being walking through something difficult, and you will not live here forever. Because you will not.

Identity beyond depression means remembering who you were before you started believing the lie, and clearly visualizing the better, stronger *you* that will emerge after. It means remembering your laugh before it got quiet. Remember your dreams before they got buried under survival. It means remembering how creative you were before you got tired. Your confidence is returning daily and life will not be able crush you again. Depression made you forget yourself. It makes you forget what

83

you've already overcome and are allowed to move forward from. It makes you forget how strong you are. But you have evidence that you are resilient. Reading this book proves that you are committed to working on yourself. You are developing the endurance needed to kick the butt of depression. You are not weak. You are very strong and on your way to full restoration.

Rewriting the story also means forgiving yourself for what you didn't know. Some of you are carrying shame for not healing faster. Still downing yourself for choosing the wrong person. Shaming yourself for staying too long. We have all been there. We have all made bad decisions. We must experience life, the good the bad and the ugly, in order to learn. Red flags are not always obvious. The truth is, you were doing the best you could with what you had at the time. You cannot build a new identity while punishing yourself for your old one. You must learn to look at yourself with compassion and love. You must learn to speak to yourself like you would speak to someone you love. Because that is precisely what you deserve.

Depression makes you focus on everything you are not. But healing invites you to focus on what you are becoming. You are becoming wiser. You are becoming more honest. You are becoming stronger in a deeper way. You are now self-aware. You are creating positive emotional tools to assist you if depression tries to show up again. You are becoming more protective of your peace and putting your mental health first. You are becoming more spiritually grounded. You are becoming someone who knows the difference between real peace and performance. you are now someone who knows the difference between love and unhealthy attachment. Depression tried to shrink your value and steal your self-worth, but healing will expand you into your true purpose.

84

Sometimes rewriting the story means changing the way you speak about yourself out loud. Depression often tries to make you speak in a way that keeps you trapped. It wants your words to be final. It wants your words to be hopeless and harsh. But your words have power. They are energy and create the atmosphere. Your words shape your mindset. Your words affect your nervous system. Your words are not just describing your life, they are directing your life. When you begin to speak with intention, you begin to shift your inner world. That is why recognizing that you are actively participating in negative thinking is half the battle won. Many people spend years in denial, completely oblivious to the fact that 90% of the thoughts they allow in their mind daily are not positive. This can lead to depression. Mankind as a whole needs to realize how important our thoughts are to the quality of life we live. Mind is all and thoughts are everything. It all begins with a single thought. God gave us the ability to manifest any kind of life we desire, but the first step to creating a great life is thinking about one. **What you Think About you Bring About.!**

That is why it is imperative that we take time to monitor our thoughts. I want you to begin to think of your thoughts as seeds and the mind being the garden. The garden will produce pre-cisely what we plant. If we plant thoughts of a stressful, sickly, impoverished life in the garden of our minds, that is exactly what we will get. Because many of us don't realize how often we actually have negative, fear-based thoughts, conforming to this positive way of thinking may seem challenging at first. But anything you do continuously will eventually become a habit, and this is a habit that is well worth developing. Rewriting the story is not about pretending nothing hurts, and it is not about denying your struggle. This means you refuse to worship it. You refuse to give it the final say. You refuse to let it be the loudest voice in your life.

Identity beyond depression also means you stop living as if you are permanently damaged. You may have scars, but scars are evidence of healing, not evidence of defeat. Scars mean you survived. Scars mean the wound closed. Scars mean your body found a way to repair itself. Spiritually, scars can become testimony. They can become proof that God carried you, even when you were at your lowest. Depression wants your scars to become shame, but healing turns your scars into strength. You are not the worst thing you've been through. You are not the worst thing you've ever thought. You are not the most painful moment of your life. You are not what someone else did to you. You are not what you lost. You are not what went wrong. You are not your diagnosis. You are not your depression. You are you, the real you, the magnificent spiritual you. The you that still has purpose. The you that still has value. The you that still has a bright light inside of them. The you that still has a future. Even if it feels far away right now, it is still yours.

That is why rewriting the story is not a one-time decision. It is a daily practice. It is waking up and choosing not to agree with the lie. It is noticing the old narrative and replacing it with truth. It is catching the voice of shame and speaking love and compassion instead. It is remembering that healing is not linear and refusing to quit because of a setback. It is learning how to talk to yourself like someone worth saving, because you are. The truth is, depression may have introduced itself to you, but it does not get to become your name. It does not get to sit on the throne of your identity, nor write the definition of who you are. You are not the darkness you walked through, you are the light that kept showing up anyway. You are not the breakdown, you are the breakthrough that is being built inside you right now. Even if you can't see the full picture yet, heaven can. God can. Your future can. Your story is still unfolding, and the parts that hurt are not proof that you're doomed. They are proof that you're still alive, still chosen, still being shaped, still becoming who god intended for you to be.

So from this chapter forward, let this be your declaration, quiet or loud, whispered or spoken, tearful or confident:

I am not depression. I am not my worst thoughts. I am not my lowest season. I am not what tried to take me out. I am the one who stayed and got up to face another day. I am the one who not only survived, but thrived. I am the one who is healing and rising. I don't have to wait until everything feels perfect to claim my identity. I can claim it right now, in the middle of the process, in the middle of the rebuilding, in the middle of the fog, because my identity is not based on what I feel today. My identity is based on who I truly am, and who God created me to be.

10

Peace on Purpose: Designing a Life That Protects Your Mind

Peace is not something you stumble into. Peace is something you choose, build, and protect. After depression, you learn that you cannot afford a life that constantly drains you. You cannot afford to treat your mind like it will just "figure it out" while you keep pouring yourself into everything and everyone. Healing teaches you that your joy needs support. Your peace needs structure. Your mind needs safety. If you don't design your life with intention, life will design it for you, and it will not always choose what is healthiest.

Peace on purpose begins when you stop living in reaction mode. Depression keeps you reacting, reacting to people, reacting to stress, reacting to memories, reacting to triggers, reacting to pressure, reacting to the fear of disappointing others. But when you begin to design your life, you start responding instead of reacting. You begin making decisions based on what nurtures you, not just what demands you. You begin asking yourself different questions. Not "What do they need from me?" but "What do I need to stay well?" Not "How do I keep everybody happy?" but "How do I keep myself stable?" Not "How do I push through?" but "How do I live in a way that supports my healing?"

A life that protects your mind is not a perfect life. It's a wise life. It's a life that understands your nervous system has limits. It's a life that respects your emotions instead of ignoring them until they explode. It's a life that values rest as much as productivity. It's a life that makes room for silence, for breath, for God, for clarity. Because if you never make space to process, you will eventually pay for it in overwhelm, and overwhelm is one of depression's favorite doors.

Peace on purpose also means deciding what kind of energy gets access to you. Not everyone deserves front-row seats to your life. Not every conversation deserves your attention. Not every opinion deserves a place in your mind. There are people who love chaos. People who thrive on drama. People who don't respect boundaries. People who keep you anxious. People who always have a crisis. People who only call when they need something. In the past, you may have tolerated that because you wanted to be kind, wanted to be supportive, wanted to be understood. But healing teaches you that kindness without boundaries becomes self-abandonment. Designing a peaceful life means you choose relationships that nourish you, not relationships that constantly keep you in survival mode.

Sometimes protecting your mind means simplifying. Depression can come from carrying too much for too long. Too many commitments. Too many responsibilities. Too many emotional burdens. Too many roles. Too much noise. Too much pressure. You cannot heal in the same pace that broke you. You cannot recover while living like you are running from something. Sometimes peace on purpose looks like slowing down and giving yourself permission to live at a more humane speed. The world might clap for hustle, but your mental health claps for balance.

Designing a life that protects your mind means creating routines that soothe you. Not rigid rules that feel like punishment, but gentle rhythms that feel like support. A morning that doesn't start with panic. A night that doesn't end with chaos. Time to breathe. Time to pray. Time to be still. Time to feed your body. Time to move your body. Time to check in with your emotions. Time to do something that brings you joy without guilt. When you create rhythm, your nervous system begins to trust your life again. Your mind begins to feel safer. Your emotions become less extreme because your system is no longer constantly startled by disorder.

Peace on purpose also means you learn how to protect your mind from you. That might sound strange, but it matters. Because sometimes the loudest enemy is the inner voice that keeps criticizing you—the voice that keeps replaying the past, the voice that keeps predicting failure, the voice that keeps telling you you're behind, the voice that keeps comparing. Healing requires you to become aware of how you talk to yourself. A peaceful life includes a peaceful inner environment. You cannot build peace externally while declaring war on yourself internally. You deserve a mind that feels like home, not a place where you get attacked all day.

Spiritually, protecting your mind is sacred. Your mind is where you interpret life. Your mind is where you hear God. Your mind is where you make meaning. If your mind is constantly under assault, it becomes harder to recognize truth. It becomes harder to trust your instincts. It becomes harder to feel hope. That is why peace on purpose is more than self-care. It is stewardship. It is you honoring what God gave you. It is you valuing your life enough to protect it. It is you saying, "I will not keep entertaining thoughts and environments that destroy me."

A peaceful life also includes joy. Not the kind of joy that depends on everything going right, but the kind of joy that comes from living aligned, living honest, living with self-respect, living with boundaries, living with faith, living with rest. Depression tries to convince you joy is childish, joy is risky, joy will be taken away, so you might as well not reach for it. But joy is not a luxury. Joy is medicine. Joy is strength. Joy is a sign of life. When you begin making room for joy again, you are telling your nervous system, "We are safe enough to feel good."

Protecting your mind also means planning for hard days. Not from fear, but from wisdom. You don't wait for the storm to build a roof. You don't wait for the spiral to decide you'll start caring for yourself. Peace on purpose includes knowing your warning signs and respecting them. It includes knowing when to rest, when to reach out, when to pause, when to say no, when to step back, when to pray, when to get professional support. A designed life has support systems built into it. It has safeguards. It has accountability. It has a plan that reminds you: even on hard days, you are not starting over, you are continuing.

And one of the most powerful parts of designing a peaceful life is realizing you are allowed to change. You are allowed to do things differently than you used to. You are allowed to choose a new environment. You are allowed to choose new habits. You are allowed to choose new relationships. You are allowed to choose yourself. You are allowed to stop trying to be the version of you that pleased everyone but was dying inside. Healing gives you permission to become who you actually are, not who depression told you you were, not who trauma forced you to be, not who everyone expected you to be. You get to build your life around your healing, and that is not selfish. That is survival turned into wisdom.

Peace on purpose is not a one-time decision. It is a daily practice. It is waking up and choosing what supports your mind. It is noticing what drains you and adjusting. It is listening to your body and responding with care. It is honoring your limits without shame. It is choosing faith over fear. It is choosing rest over burnout. It is choosing truth over performance. It is choosing you, again and again, until it becomes your lifestyle.

You deserve a life that doesn't require you to recover from it. You deserve mornings that don't feel like dread. You deserve relationships that don't feel like survival. You deserve a mind that has room to breathe. The more you design your life with peace in mind, the more your healing becomes stable, sustainable, and real.

You made it to the end of this book, and that alone is proof of something powerful. It means there is still life in you. It means the part of you that wants peace is stronger than the part of you that wants to quit. Depression may have tried to silence you, shrink you, and convince you that you were alone, but you are still here. You are still reading. You are still reaching. That is not small, that is courage in its purest form.

Let this be your reminder that healing is real, even when it is slow. Healing is real when you get up and your heart still feels heavy. Healing is real when you choose to breathe instead of break. Healing is real when you set a boundary, tell the truth, ask for help, rest without guilt, and try again after a hard day. Your progress is not measured by perfection. It is measured by persistence. It is measured by the decision to keep choosing yourself, even when your emotions are loud and unruly, even when your past tries to pull you back in, even when your mind tells you it won't get better. It will! Keep choosing yourself daily.

There will be moments in your life when the darkness tries to revisit you, not because you failed, but because life happens. When it does, I want you to remember what you have learned here. You are not powerless in your own mind. You are not your worst day. You are not your lowest season. You are not what happened to you. You are not what you lost. You are not what you fear. You are a whole human being in process, and your future is allowed to be brighter than your past. You have tools now. You have wisdom now. You have a voice now. You have the right to protect your peace like your life depends on it—because it does.

It's time to celebrate your new life, where you are the master of your fate. Learning how to control your thoughts is the catalyst to that. This is the beginning of a great life. It's all uphill from here. If you utilize the positive mind tools I speak of in this book, you absolutely cannot fail. You can win the war against negative thinking every single time. You have a magnificent future ahead of you. I am excited for you. Let every new season in your life be a winning season. Winning the battle over negative thinking will be one of the most significant and useful skills you will ever master. It will change your life.

It's one thing to learn to win the war against negative thinking yourself. It is a whole different challenge to teach it to others. However, that is exactly what it will take in order for the generations that follow us to be empowered enough to make an impactful difference in the world. We must teach each child about the infinite power within themselves.

I have spent numerous years fighting the mental enemy that

made me question my worth. Those days are now over. I am great, and so are you. I have won the war, and you can win it too. There is no greater feeling than sincere, authentic self-love.

The world is yours. You have the power to design it any way that you wan, through your thoughts and your expansive imagination. Use your beautiful mind to create heaven here on Earth.

I am creating a world of love, respect, and peace for myself. When I close my eyes and imagine, I see a life filled with people who sincerely love me and always have my best interests at heart. Each of you can create the same for yourselves. We do not have to suffer during this life experience. Happiness is possible for us all.

We cannot rid the world of negative people, they will always exist, but we can limit access to anyone who is not radiating kindness and love. You have the starring role in your story. Take control over how your life turns out. Leave nothing to chance.

Implement the positive practices you have learned in this book and begin to enjoy everything that this amazing world has to offer. You can't change the chaos in the world, but you can learn to calm the chaos in your mind. In the endless battle of negative and positive, take purposeful steps to ensure that you win the war every time.

So as you close this book, don't just hope for a better life. Create One! Decide that your mind deserves safety. Decide that your heart deserves gentleness. Decide that your body deserves rest. Decide that your spirit deserves abundant love and light. Decide that you will not make a permanent decision during a temporary storm. The storm is sure to pass.

Please keep building your life on purpose, one day at a time, one small win at a time, one brave choice at a time. Because you were never created to live under a cloud forever. You were never created to be surrounded by the fog of depression. You were created to breathe deeply, smile brightly, and to heal and rise up and feel joy and love again. No matter how long it takes, no matter how many times you have to start over, your life is worth fighting for. Never give up!

Now here is your call to action: protect your peace like it is sacred, because it is. Stop making room for what makes you smaller. Stop giving unlimited access to people who keep you anxious, confused, and depleted. Stop rehearsing the same hurt until it becomes your identity. Make your healing a lifestyle, daily, intentional and consistent. Decide what you will no longer tolerate or entertain. Decide what you will no longer carry. Back that decision up with action, even if you are afraid and your voice shakes, even if your heart pounds, even if you have to choose yourself a hundred times before it feels natural. Do not Stop!

Please hear me when I say this: you are not too far gone. There is always hope. You are not too damaged to get through this. You are not too complicated. You are not "stuck like this forever." You are a living, breathing miracle in motion, and the fact that you are still here, waking up every morning, means your story is not finished.

If you've been surviving on the edge, if you've been smiling while suffering, if you've been telling everyone "I'm good" while your soul has been crying out, let this be the moment you stop negotiating with darkness and bring yourself back to the beautiful light. Let this be the moment you speak, pray, rest, get support, take your medication if prescribed, follow your doctor's instructions, use the affirmation tools, monitor your thoughts, do the internal work needed to keep going, because your life is worth that kind of fight.

So go ahead and close this book, but don't close the door on your healing. Take what you learned in this book and apply it to your everyday life. Reshaping the mindset is a process that requires consistency. Write the affirmations down and read them daily. Record them and listen to them nightly as you are drifting off to sleep. Set your boundaries and only let positive, uplifting people in your circle. Tell the truth to yourself and acknowledge when you are feeling bad. Make the Doctors appointment. Take the walk outside and feel the warmth of the sun. Drink plenty of water and get a lot of peaceful rest. Say no without guilt and put yourself first. Say yes to your new amazing future. If depression tries to creep back in and act like it owns you, I want you to remember the title of this book and let it become your attitude, your energy, your declaration: *Start* ***Kicking Depression in the Butt***. Because you were created to live a happy, fulfilling life because you are an Extraordinary Being!

About the Author

SaBrina Fisher Reece was once known throughout California as *"The Braid Queen."*

For over twenty-six years, she owned and operated the legendary **Braids By SaBrina**, a celebrated salon and school on Adams Boulevard in Los Angeles. It became the largest and most influential braiding establishment in the city, a place where artistry, empowerment, and community beautifully intertwined.

As SaBrina stepped into the second half of her life, she felt a divine calling to share the deeper story behind her success, a journey of faith, transformation, and inner peace. What began as a career of creativity evolved into a life of purpose. She now inspires others through her writing and motivational speaking, guiding people toward healing and self-discovery.

She is also the of author of *My Spiritual Smile, Your Mind is Magic, How to Make More Money in 2026, My Internet Dating Journals for men and women, Perfectly Positive, Become Your own cheerleader, When I Say "I Am", The Family Fun night Cookbook and many more, they are each one* a reflection of her own awakening.

SaBrina is a devoted mother of four, **Justin, Joi, Jayden, and Journey,** and a proud grandmother to **Raiden Jesse** and **Rio Jordan**. Her greatest joy is watching them, and all those she teaches, awaken to their divine potential.

Her passion for sound and frequency has led her to explore the healing power of **crystal sound bowls, tuning forks, and flow chimes,** tools that help harmonize the body, mind, and spirit. Yet, she reminds her students and readers that there is no single path to peace. Every person's journey is sacred, and every method of connecting with the Divine is worthy.

Now residing in the enchanting landscapes of **New Mexico, "The Land of Enchantment"** - SaBrina offers **Sound Vibration Sessions** that invite others to slow down, breathe deeply, and reconnect with their higher selves.

Her message is simple, timeless, and true:

"We were each born with divine energy, a God-given power to create, to heal, and to live fully.

The goal is not perfection, but peace.

The journey is not to escape life, but to embrace it, vibrantly, joyfully, and in harmony with the soul."

Also by SaBrina Fisher Reece

SaBrina Fisher Reece was once known throughout California as *"The Braid Queen."*

For over twenty-six years, she owned and operated the legendary **Braids By SaBrina**, a celebrated salon and school on Adams Boulevard in Los Angeles. It became the largest and most influential braiding establishment in the city, a place where artistry, empowerment, and community beautifully intertwined.

As SaBrina stepped into the second half of her life, she felt a divine calling to share the deeper story behind her success, a journey of faith, transformation, and inner peace. What began as a career of creativity evolved into a life of purpose. She now inspires others through her writing and motivational speaking, guiding people toward healing and self-discovery.

She is the author of *My Spiritual Smile*, *How to Get Exactly what You Want from God*, *Your Mind is Magic*, and *Perfectly Positive*, *Living Life on a Higher Frequency*, *When I Say "I Am"* each one a reflection of her own awakening. Her books are true gifts to the world.

SaBrina is a devoted mother of four - **Justin, Joi, Jayden, and Journey** - and a proud grandmother to **Raiden Jesse** and **Rio Jordan**. Her greatest joy is watching them, and all those she teaches, awaken to their divine potential.

Her passion for sound and frequency has led her to explore the healing power of **crystal sound bowls, tuning forks, and flow chimes** - tools that help harmonize the body, mind, and spirit. Yet, she reminds her students and readers that there is no single path to peace. Every person's journey is sacred, and every method of connecting with the Divine is worthy.

"The Land of Enchantment" - SaBrina offers **Sound Vibration Sessions** that invite others to slow down, breathe deeply, and reconnect with their higher selves.

Her message is simple, timeless, and true:

"We were each born with Divine Energy - a God-given power to create, to heal, and to live a full successful life.

The goal is not perfection, but peace and happiness.

The journey is not to escape life, but to embrace it - vibrantly, joyfully, and in harmony with the soul."

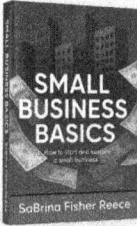

Small Business Basics: How to Start and Sustain a Small Business

Small Business Basics is the book every new entrepreneur wishes they had on day one. In this powerful, real-world guide, SaBrina Fisher Reece - founder of Braids By SaBrina, A New Vision Dreadlock Studio, Just-In Time Barber Shop, and Inked 4 Life Tattoo Studio - shares the exact blueprint she used to build and sustain multiple successful businesses over 30 years.

This is not theory.

This is not fluff.

This is lived experience - straight from a woman who started with nothing but grit, faith, and a gift from God.

Inside these pages, SaBrina teaches you how to:

✔ Start your business with confidence

✔ Build structure, systems, and strong policies

✔ Attract clients with real marketing (not gimmicks)

✔ Lead with authority, heart, and integrity

✔ Set prices that reflect your worth

✔ Stay consistent, disciplined, and profitable

✔ Avoid the common mistakes that destroy small businesses

SaBrina has hired, trained, and mentored more than **1,700 employees**, survived betrayals, grown through heartbreak, and built an empire that became a household name in Los Angeles. Her lessons are raw, honest, spiritual, and rooted in the belief that **anyone can build a business - if they have the courage to start and the discipline to stay consistent.**

Whether you're launching your first idea, fixing a struggling business, or leveling up your brand, this book gives you the mindset, strategy, and motivation to succeed.

Your dream is possible.
Your vision is valid.
Your future is waiting.
Start today. Not tomorrow.

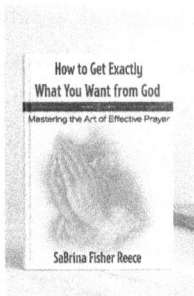

How to Get Exactly What You Want from God

How to Get Exactly What You Want From God shows you how to pray with results. Inside, you'll learn how to make specific requests, build the faith needed to sustain them, and match your thoughts and emotions to the outcome you want. SaBrina teaches you how to interrupt negative self-talk, eliminate doubt, and step into a mindset that attracts divine answers quickly and clearly. This is your guide to intentional prayer, spiritual alignment, and receiving blessings without hesitation.

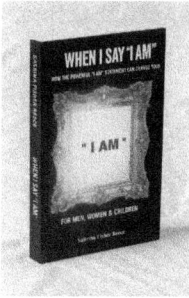

When I Say "I Am"

What you say after "I Am" has the power to shape your entire life.

In *When I Say "I Am"*, SaBrina Fisher Reece reveals the sacred and scientific power of spoken identity. Blending spiritual truth, biblical wisdom, and universal law, this transformational book teaches readers how their words are not just communication—but creation. Every "I Am" statement becomes a command to the subconscious, a signal to the universe, and a declaration to the spiritual realm.

Drawing from scripture, including God's revelation of "**I AM**" as the eternal source of being, SaBrina shows how the same creative force lives within each of us. Through emotionally moving insight, practical affirmations, and deep spiritual awareness, readers learn how to shift from fear-based language to faith-based declarations that activate healing, confidence, abundance, and purpose.

This book will help you:

Break negative identity patterns

Reprogram limiting beliefs

Speak life instead of fear

Align your words with divine promise

Use "**I Am**" as a daily tool for transformation

More than motivation, *When I Say "I Am"* is a blueprint for conscious creation. It reminds you that your voice is powerful, your identity is sacred, and your words are always working— either for you or against you.

If you are ready to stop speaking survival and start speaking destiny, this book will show you how to command your life with intention, faith, and divine authority—one "I Am" at a time.

Become Your own Cheerleader

Become Your Own Cheerleader: Moving Forward in Life Without the Support of Others is a powerful, honest guide for anyone who has ever felt unseen, unsupported, or overlooked by the very people they hoped would cheer the loudest.

In this deeply personal and transformational book, SaBrina Fisher Reece invites readers into her life story, one shaped by early abandonment, profound loss, resilience, and hard-earned self-trust. From surviving childhood trauma and the murder of the grandmother who raised her, to building businesses, writing books, and leading without consistent support, SaBrina reveals what happens when you stop waiting for applause and start standing firmly in your own worth.

This is not a book about bitterness. It is a book about liberation.

Through raw storytelling and hard truths, you will learn why some people cannot clap for you, how to stop taking silence personally, and why your worth is never up for a vote. You will discover how to release the need for validation, acknowledge the few who truly support you, and become the voice you once needed to hear from others.

Each chapter builds toward one essential truth: the most powerful support you will ever receive must come from within.

Whether you are navigating family disappointment, friendship distance, professional invisibility, or emotional independence, **Become Your Own Cheerleader** offers clarity, comfort, and courage. It teaches you how to keep going when no one is watching, how to celebrate yourself without guilt, and how to live boldly without waiting for permission.

This book is for the strong ones who got strong too early.

For the ones who kept showing up.

For the ones who learned how to clap for themselves.

If you are ready to stop waiting for approval and start living like you believe in you, this book is for you.

Over 50 and Still Fine - Looking to Date Again

Dating after fifty is not about lowering your standards, settling, or giving up on love. It's about learning how to date with clarity, emotional control, and confidence.

In this candid, insightful, and often humorous book, **SaBrina Fisher Reece** takes readers inside her real-life dating experiences and the powerful lessons they revealed. Through personal stories, emotional turning points, and hard-earned wisdom, she explores modern dating through the lens of maturity, self-respect, and growth.

This is not a guide filled with rigid rules or unrealistic fairy tales. Instead, it is a compassionate conversation for women who have lived, loved, healed, and are still open to connection. From recognizing red flags without becoming cynical, to balancing openness with boundaries, SaBrina shows how emotional control becomes the foundation for healthy dating and lasting peace.

You'll learn how to:

Identify emotional instability and red flags early without judgment

Stay lighthearted and open while protecting your peace

Navigate modern dating, including online dating and new social formats

Release fear, bitterness, and old attachment patterns

Date with intention instead of emotional exhaustion

This book is for women who are done chasing potential, managing chaos, or confusing attention with love. It's for women who want joy, safety, laughter, and connection without sacrificing themselves in the process.

Whether you're newly dating, taking a break, or simply rethinking how you approach love, this book will remind you that your heart is seasoned, your standards are valid, and love has not passed you by.

Dating didn't fail you.

You evolved.

And love can evolve with you.

Profound- Activate -Think - Live 4 book Series

Introduction to the Profound Series

This series was not written to convince you of anything.

It was written to remind you of something.

For most of my life, I searched for answers the same way many people do. I looked outward. I prayed, studied, worked, endured, and tried to become better by force. I believed growth meant effort alone and that transformation required suffering. I was taught, as many of us are, what to believe, what to question, and what to avoid.

What I did not realize at the time was that I was not missing faith.

I was missing understanding.

The *Profound Series* was born from a deeply personal journey of self-discovery, healing, and expansion. It is the result of decades of reading ancient texts, studying metaphysical teachings, reflecting on spiritual principles, and most importantly, applying this wisdom in real life. This series is not meant to replace religion, tradition, or belief systems. It is meant to widen the lens.

Religion offers structure, community, and devotion. Ancient wisdom offers context, depth, and responsibility. Together, they reveal something powerful: that you are not separate from the divine, and you were never meant to live disconnected from your inner power.

This series exists because I discovered that much of what we are seeking has already been known for centuries. Long before modern psychology, neuroscience, or self-help, ancient philosophers, mystics, teachers, and spiritual scholars understood the relationship between thought, emotion, consciousness, and reality. They understood that the mind is creative, that belief shapes experience, and that life responds to awareness.

The first book, **Profound**, is about remembering. It is about gathering ancient wisdom and recognizing truths that may feel familiar even if you are encountering them for the first time. This is the awakening stage. The moment when something inside you says, "There is more."

The second book, **Activate**, is about embodiment. Knowledge alone does not change a life. It must be practiced. This book moves wisdom from the intellect into daily living. It teaches you how to tap into the divine energy within you and apply what you have learned in practical, grounded ways.

The third book, **Think**, is about mastery of the mind. Thought is not passive. It is creative. This book guides you in becoming aware of your inner dialogue, understanding how thoughts shape experience, and learning how to consciously direct the mental patterns that influence your life.

The fourth book, **Live**, is about integration. This is where knowledge, practice, and awareness become who you are. You no longer strive to be aligned. You live aligned. You move through the world with clarity, compassion, and confidence, embodying the wisdom you have gained.

Together, these four books form a complete journey.

Awakening. Activation. Mastery. Expression.

This is not a quick fix. It is not spiritual bypassing. It is not about perfection. It is about responsibility. Responsibility for your thoughts. Responsibility for your emotional state. Responsibility for the energy you bring into the world.

The world does not need more information. It needs more

conscious people. People who are self-aware. People who understand cause and effect at the level of thought and emotion. People who can pause, reflect, and respond instead of react. People who live from inner alignment rather than fear.

You were never meant to live small, disconnected, or powerless. You were meant to participate in your own evolution.

This series is an invitation. Not to abandon what you believe, but to expand it. Not to follow me, but to follow your own inner knowing. Not to search endlessly outside yourself, but to reconnect with what has always been within you.

If you are reading this, you are ready.

Ready to remember.

Ready to activate.

Ready to master your mind.

Ready to live fully.

Welcome to the journey.

How Do I Control My Emotions?

When Anger, Rage, and Impulsive Behavior Is Destroying Your Life

Anger does not make you powerful. It makes you reactive. Unchecked reactions can quietly dismantle your relationships, your health, your career, and your peace.

In **How Do I Control My Emotions?**, author and transformational voice **SaBrina Fisher Reece** takes you on a deeply honest journey through emotional self-mastery. Drawing from her own lived experiences as a business owner, leader, and woman who once wore anger as armor, SaBrina exposes the real roots of rage, impulsive behavior, and emotional outbursts—and shows you how to take your power back.

This book is not about suppressing emotions or pretending everything is fine. It is about understanding why you react the way you do, identifying hidden triggers tied to abandonment, trauma, and unmet needs, and learning how to pause, choose, and respond with intention instead of regret.

Inside these pages, you will learn:

Why anger feels justified in the moment but costs you in the long run

How unhealed pain disguises itself as control, dominance, or intensity

The difference between reacting and responding

Why emotional discipline is a form of self-respect

How to stop letting your past control your present

Written with compassion, clarity, and accountability, this book is a call to action for anyone tired of apologizing, repairing damage, or living with the consequences of emotional explosions. If you are ready to stop being ruled by anger and start living from self-control, awareness, and peace, this book will meet you exactly where you are.

You cannot control other people.

But you can always control **you**.

And that changes everything.

Catch and Cast

Reversing Negative Thinking Patterns is an empowering guide to taking control of the mind and ending the cycle of unnecessary emotional suffering.

In this deeply personal and compassionate book, self help author SaBrina Fisher Reece introduces a simple yet transformative approach to mental healing. Drawing from her own lived experience with depression, post traumatic stress, abandonment, and loss, she teaches readers how to stop negative thoughts in their tracks and replace them with thoughts that support peace, self worth, and emotional freedom.

At the heart of the book is the Recognize, Reject, Replace system, a practical framework designed to help readers become aware of harmful thought patterns, consciously refuse them, and intentionally choose healthier alternatives. Rather than encouraging suppression or denial of pain, this method emphasizes awareness, choice, and responsibility, allowing healing to unfold without shame or judgment.

Written in a warm, loving, and conversational voice, **Catch and Cast** reassures readers that negative thoughts do not mean they are broken. It shows how the mind, while powerful, does not have to be in control. Through insight, reflection, and daily practice, readers learn that suffering does not have to be permanent and that peace is possible, even after deep trauma.

This book is for anyone who feels trapped by their thoughts, overwhelmed by recurring mental images, or unaware that they have the power to choose what lives in their inner world. It offers hope without false promises and guidance without condemnation.

Catch and Cast reminds readers that while pain may be part of life, prolonged suffering is not. Healing begins in the mind, and the tools to achieve it are already within reach.

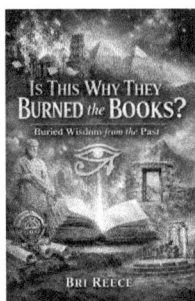

Is This Why They Burned The Books?
(EBOOK)
Buried Wisdom from the Past

What if the most powerful knowledge was never destroyed... only buried?

Across history, libraries have burned, philosophers have been silenced, and ancient civilizations have disappeared. Yet fragments of their wisdom continue to surface in unexpected places. In sacred geometry carved into stone. In healing traditions rooted in the earth. In philosophies that challenge us to master the mind. In spiritual teachings that insist the kingdom is within.

In *Is This Why They Burned the Books?*, Bri Reece takes readers on a deeply personal and thought provoking journey through ancient Egypt, Peru, and Greece, exploring the possibility that humanity once understood more about consciousness, energy, and inner power than we acknowledge today.

Drawing from travel experiences inside the Great Pyramid of Giza, meditation above Machu Picchu, and reflections in Delphi and Meteora, this book bridges ancient civilizations with modern self awareness. It asks bold but balanced questions:

What did our ancestors know about the mind?

Why do certain ideas about human potential keep resurfacing across centuries?

Are we operating at only a fraction of our true capacity?

What does evolving to a higher self actually look like?

This is not a conspiracy book. It is a curiosity book.

It does not attack religion. It expands perspective.

It does not claim certainty. It invites exploration.

Through thoughtful reflection on ancient wisdom, energy,

grounding, inner discipline, and the vastness of the universe, Bri Reece offers readers something far more valuable than answers. She offers responsibility. The responsibility to think deeply, to seek humbly, and to remember that human potential is far from exhausted.

If you have ever felt that there is more to this life than routine and repetition...

If you are a seeker who questions without arrogance...

If you sense that buried wisdom is waiting to be rediscovered...

This book is for you.

The fire may have burned the pages.

But the wisdom remains.

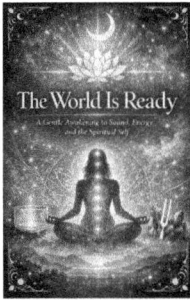

The World Is Ready EBOOK

A Gentle Awakening to Sound, Energy, and the Spiritual Self is a compassionate invitation for those who sense there is more to life than what they were taught to see, yet still wish to honor their faith, their upbringing, and their reverence for God.

Written for readers raised within structured religious traditions, this book offers a safe and respectful bridge into spiritual practices that support balance, healing, and inner awareness. It reassures the reader that exploring sound healing, breathwork, meditation, grounding, and energy awareness is not a betrayal of faith, but a natural expansion of it.

Through deeply personal experiences, including recovery from major surgery supported by sound, private sound healing sessions, and sacred encounters in spiritual sites across the world, the author gently illustrates how ancient practices and modern understanding meet. From binaural beats and tuning forks to healing crystals, chakras, breath as life force, and the quiet power of the mind, each chapter unfolds with warmth, clarity, and emotional honesty.

This book does not preach, persuade, or pressure. Instead, it speaks softly to the soul, honoring curiosity while dissolving fear. It recognizes that spirituality does not belong to one religion, culture, or language, but lives within the shared human experience of seeking peace, connection, and meaning.

The World Is Ready is for anyone who has ever felt drawn to spiritual exploration but hesitated out of loyalty, doubt, or uncertainty. It affirms that spiritual practices are not witchcraft or rebellion, but tools of awareness that help us return to balance, regulate the nervous system, and remember our true nature.

This is not a call to abandon belief.

It is an invitation to remember who you are.

The world is ready.

Pressure Down Plates

High blood pressure does not mean giving up flavor.

It does not mean bland food, boring meals, or feeling restricted at the dinner table. It means learning how to cook smarter, season differently, and nourish your body in a way that supports your heart.

In *Pressure Down Plates*, you will discover delicious, satisfying meals designed to help lower blood pressure naturally-without sacrificing taste. This cookbook focuses on simple ingredients, practical swaps, and flavorful combinations that make heart-healthy eating feel enjoyable instead of overwhelming.

Inside you'll find:

Low-sodium meals packed with flavor

Smart seasoning alternatives that don't rely on excess salt

Simple recipes for busy weeknights

Wholesome ingredients that support heart health

Easy dishes the whole family will love

Whether you are newly diagnosed, managing long-term hypertension, or simply wanting to be proactive about your health, this book gives you meals you can actually look forward to eating.

Taking care of your heart should feel empowering-not limiting.

Lower the pressure. Lift your plates. Enjoy your food again.

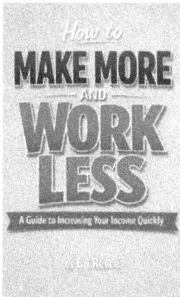

How to Make More and Work Less
A Guide to Increasing Your Income Quickly is not another hustle book filled with recycled advice or unrealistic promises. It is a grounded, compassionate guide for people who have worked hard, played by the rules, and still found themselves facing financial uncertainty in a changing economy.

Written from lived experience, this book speaks directly to adults who are tired of surviving and ready to build a life that includes peace, stability, and abundance. With honesty and warmth, Bri Reece shows readers how to stop trading endless hours for diminishing returns and start creating income through their existing skills, knowledge, and life experience.

Blending practical insight with heartfelt encouragement, this book explores how to turn what you already know into income, how old school marketing still works in a digital world, and how teaching, writing, and speaking can create leverage without burnout. Most importantly, it addresses the mindset shift required to move from constant stress to sustainable freedom, reminding readers that struggle may have been part of their journey, but it was never meant to be their forever.

This book is for anyone who has worried quietly about bills, felt overlooked by a changing economy, or wondered if it was too late to start again. It offers clarity, hope, and real options for making more money while reclaiming time, dignity, and joy.

If you are ready to believe in possibility again and build a life that supports you instead of drains you, this book meets you exactly where you are and gently shows you what is still possible.

www.ingramcontent.com/pod-product-compliance
Lightning Source LLC
LaVergne TN
LVHW011207080426
835508LV00007B/650